FAITH,

FOOLISHNESS,

OR

PRESUMPTION?

by

Frederick K.C. Price

HARRISON HOUSE
P.O. Box 35035
Tulsa, Okla. 74135

(All Scripture quotations from *King James Version* of the
Bible, unless otherwise stated.)

Cover Design
by
Cygnet

ISBN 0-89274-103-1
Printed in United States of America
Copyright© 1979 Frederick K. C. Price
All Rights Reserved

Table of Contents

1

Laying The Foundation

There are many people doing many things under the guise of *Faith*, when in fact, it is not Faith at all: it is *Foolishness*, and in most cases, it is *Presumption*. We want to deal with this important matter, and bring it out as clearly as we can, so that those who are desirous to walk in line with the Word of God will actually be walking consistently with the Word, and not in *Foolishness*, nor *Presumption*. We will talk about *Faith*, *Foolishness*, or *Presumption*? Which is it?

FAITH IS A WAY OF LIFE

We read in Habakkuk 2:4, "Behold, his soul which is lifted up is not upright in him; but the just shall live by his faith." This is the part of the verse that I want you to see: But the just shall live by his faith. How? ". . . the just shall live by faith." Well, if the just shall live by faith, then *faith* must be *a way of life*.

Too many have thought that faith was an instant, "get—rich—quick—scheme," a panacea for all your ills: a parachute to instantly bail you out of a problem in which you may be presently embroiled.

Faith is a way of life. It is a way of living. It is not an "instant-get-rich-quick-scheme." *It is a way of life*. He said, "The just shall live by faith." Paul is actually doing a takeoff from Habakkuk and other of old when he quotes the following Scripture verse. "For therein is the righteousness of God revealed from faith to faith: as it is written, the just shall live by faith" (Romans 1:17).

There is an interesting statement in the book of Galatians, and again — the emphasis is placed on a lifestyle. "The just shall live by faith." We read in chapter 3, verse 11: "But that no man is justified by the law in the sight of God, it is evident: for, The just shall live by faith." The word *just* means "one who has been justified by the blood of Jesus Christ," or more literally, "to be made or declared 'righteous.' " If you are in Christ, you have been made or declared "righteous." You are considered *one of the just*. That means then, that you should be living by faith, according to the Word of God, because it said, "The just shall live by faith."

Just to show you how important this concept — "The just shall live by faith," is in the scheme of things with God, I want you to see it as the Word of God portrays it. Hebrews 10:38 says, "Now the just shall live by faith (There it is again.): but if any man draw back, my soul shall have no pleasure in him." I will clarify something here: Because, many times words are used in common language, and they come from a traditional source, or background, and yet they have no validity or basis in the written Word of God. The word *faith* has been misused and misapplied so often, especially in the realm of what we call "religion." You have heard people ask, "What faith are you? Catholic, Protestant, or Jew?" That is really unscriptural. That is not a proper use of the biblical word *faith*. In other words; to ask somebody what faith they are is a misnomer: a misuse of the biblical word *faith*. You should be able to see that the biblical word *faith* does not mean the denomination, or church, or religion to which you belong.

We have read four passages of Scripture, and each one of them said, "The just shall live by faith." They didn't say, "The just shall live by religion." We don't need any more religions. Religion won't get you anything. It certainly won't bring you into the fellowship of Almighty God, through Jesus Christ. Christianity is not a religion. I have said it before, and I shall say it again: "We have made a religion out of Christianity, but it is not a religion." Christianity is a man — Jesus Christ. It is a way of life, and that way of life is the way of faith. "The just shall live by faith."

A familiar verse of Scripture that goes right along with what we have already read, concerning the just shall live by faith, is found in 2 Corinthians 5:7: "For we walk by faith, not by sight." Sight refers to and means *the sense realm*. We, who are in Christ, should be walking by faith, and not by what we perceive with our sensory mechanisms. Too often people have a relationship with God that is based strictly upon emotions, feelings, and sense knowledge. As long as you allow yourself the privilege of walking by your senses, you will not be able to consistently walk by faith. And if you do not walk by faith, you are not going to receive the benefits of walking by faith. God has some benefits attached to walking by faith. Most employers at least have enough common decency about them, that they don't ask somebody to work for them *for free*. They usually give them something; even if it is no more than oranges, lemons, or marbles. They usually work out some kind of agreement between the employer and the employee: an agreement that the employee will receive something from the employer for his time. If a man has enough nicety about him to do that, can't you at least believe that the Father God is not asking you to serve Him *for free* either? It would be enough just because we have received salvation, to serve Him, but thank God, He has more than salvation. He has many other things too! But we will never get into those other things until we learn how to live by faith.

YOU ARE GIVEN THE MEASURE OF FAITH

What we are doing at this point is laying a foundation. Some of these Scriptures are familiar to you: some of them are not. The whole idea is, we want to lay the foundation, and then build on it: concerning this subject, *Faith, Foolishness, Or Presumption.*

We read in Romans 12:3; "For I say, through the grace given unto me, to every man that is among you, not to think of himself more highly than he ought to think; but to think soberly, according as God hath dealt to every man the measure of faith." Now, you have to understand that the "every man" does not mean every man in the world. You have to realize that Paul was writing this letter to the Church of Jesus Christ at Rome. And of course, since we are in the same Church that the Roman Christians were in, because Jesus has only one body; He is head of the body, the Church. He is one head, and He has only one body. If we are in the Body of Christ, we have to be in the same body that the Romans were in. And thank God, we are! So when he says, "For I say, through the grace given unto me, *to every man* that is among you . . . as *God has dealt to every man the measure of faith.*" Paul means, *"every man in the family of God."* Please understand — not every man in the world, but every man in the Body of Christ. God has dealt unto every man, or given to every one of us in the Body of Christ, not *a* measure of faith, but *the* measure of faith.

The very fact that it says *the measure of faith,* is indicative of the fact that it designates a quantity, or an amount. When you say, "measure," you think of a pint, or a gallon, or something you think of as a measurement, a quantity, or degree. So when you say, "He dealt us the measure of faith," that means that we all start out with the same measure. Every person who accepts Christ as his or her personal Saviour has faith. They have to have it.

Ephesians 2:8 shows you why anyone who comes to Christ has to have faith. "For by grace (unmerited favor) are ye saved through faith; and that not of yourselves: it is the gift of God." If you are saved, you have to have faith. And if you are saved, you have that measure of faith.

HOW DOES FAITH COME TO YOU?

Paul tells us in Romans 10:17, how faith comes. "So then faith cometh by hearing, and hearing by the Word of God." Faith cometh by what? Hearing. Not by prayer, not by fasting, but faith cometh by hearing. And the reason that more Christians don't have any more faith in manifestation in their lives, is because they spend all of their lives going to churches where the Word of God is not preached in its fullness, under the unction and anointing of the Holy Spirit. And since faith cometh by hearing, and since they are not hearing the Word of God, there is no faith coming to them, and their faith is never stimulated. They have the measure because they are saved; but it never gets any stronger, because it is not being fed. The way that faith is fed is by hearing the Word of God. That is why Jesus said, "Go preach the Gospel."

This is what happened when you were saved. You heard the Word one day, somewhere, at some point in your life, and when you heard it, faith came, and you believed what you heard, and you received Jesus as Lord. You came into the family of God through the new birth. And from that moment on, that measure of faith became your personal possession. But — it is up to you to feed it, and exercise it, so that you can grow up in that measure of faith, so that it can be truly said of you, that you are a person who lives by faith.

Many people have the idea that somebody who lives by faith is supposed to be "poor-mouthing" it; the bottoms of their shoes are out; the seat of their pants out; and their old car is clinking along on two cylinders and four bald tires; they have no place to live, and no food to eat. They think to live by faith means that you have to be some kind of *weird-o*. No sir! The people who are not living by faith are the *weird-os*. They just don't know it. When you are living by faith — the faith of God — you will be on top, and if you are not on top, or moving towards the top, then you are not living by faith. You may think you are, but you are not. I have had people tell me, "Bless God, Brother Price, I have great faith, great faith! I have always believed the Bible to be the Word of God; I have gone to church and Sunday school since I was a little girl, and I have great faith."

Are you sick?

"Yes."

I thought you had great faith?

"I do."

What are you doing sick then? The Bible says, "With Jesus' stripes you were healed." If you are truly living by faith, you will have kicked sickness and disease out of your life. You can think you are doing something right, because you have good intentions, and because you are sincere about it, but you know, you can be *sincerely wrong*. I have been there! I thought I was right. I intended to be right. I wanted to be right, but I was as wrong as a three-and-one-half dollar bill. *The just shall live by faith*. We know that we have it because God has dealt us that measure.

We are laying a foundation. If you will get this into your consciousness, then you will have something to build on. We read in 2 Peter 1:1-8; "Simon Peter, a servant and an apostle of Jesus Christ, to them that have obtained like precious faith with us through the right— eousness of God and our Saviour Jesus Christ: Grace and peace be multiplied unto you through the knowledge of God, and of Jesus our Lord. According as his divine power hath given unto us all things that pertain unto life and godliness, through the knowledge of him that called us to glory and virtue." I want you to notice two things he said there, that are very important. "According as his divine power hath given unto us all things that pertain unto life and godliness." Notice, "(He) hath given them unto us." They are yours by birthright, but you will never live in them, nor will you ever enjoy them personally, until you learn how to walk and live by faith. It is the faith that causes those things which have been given to you to work in your life as an individual. Continuing with verse 4, "Whereby are given unto us exceeding great and precious promises; that by these . . . ." these what? Not just promises; not even just, great, and precious promises, but exceeding great and precious promises. ". . . that by these (these exceeding, great, and precious promises) ye might be partakers of the divine nature, having escaped the corruption that is in the world through lust. And beside this, giving all diligence, add to your faith virtue; and to virtue knowledge; And to knowledge temperance; and to temperance patience; and to patience godliness; And to godliness brotherly kindness; and to brotherly kindness charity. For if these things be in you, and abound, they make you that ye shall neither be barren nor unfruitful in the knowledge of our Lord Jesus Christ." That is shouting ground! That is out of sight! You will not be barren. But these exceeding great and precious promises work by faith. That is the very first thing he said, "And besides this, giving all diligence, add to your faith virtue!" *Add to your faith. Add to your faith. You* are supposed to do this.

FAITH, FOOLISHNESS, OR PRESUMPTION— LET'S DEFINE AND QUALIFY THESE THREE WORDS

You see that we are encouraged, yea commanded by the Word of God to live by faith. We are talking about *Faith, Foolishness, or Presumption,* and in order to talk about these things, we need to qualify our terms. The first word that we will define and qualify is the word *faith. Faith,* in its simplest definition, is "acting on what you believe." So *faith is acting on what you believe.* We are talking about *faith,* primarily, as it relates to God, but the principle works the same way in the natural world. If you say you believe something, but you fail to act on what you believe, although what you may believe may be true, historically, or scientifically, you will get no benefit out of it until you do it. You have to act on what you believe in order to get results.

"I don't understand, Brother Price, what do you mean?"

I mean this: You can take the keys to your car, pull them out of your pocket, walk out to the parking lot, climb up on the hood of your car, raise both hands heavenward, keys in one hand, and holler out at the top of your voice, "I believe that these are the keys to my car, and I believe that this is my car, and I believe that I can put these keys into the ignition of my car, and I believe that I can start my car, and I can drive home in my car." All of that may be true, friend, but you will never get home until you get off that hood, into that car, and drive home. Yet everything you said is true. It is your car, those are your keys, you can get into your car, and you can drive home. But you won't get home until you act on what you believe.

You say food will nourish your body, and keep you from starving to death. That is true, but you can starve to death in the middle of a grocery store, if you don't eat. Believing that, won't keep you from starving to death. The thing that is going to keep you from starving to death is acting on what you believe. You say that you believe it, then you do it. It is not until you act upon what you believe that it will affect your life personally. It may be true: you cannot fault the fact that it is true, but it won't affect you. And that is what you want. You want to get some benefit from it. So the simplest definition of *faith* is acting on what you believe. You say you believe the Word of God, then do the Word of God. Act on it. Relative to God, faith is acting on the Word of God: *being a doer of the Word.*

You need to have the meaning of faith very clearly entrenched in your mind, and in your spirit. You need to be very careful about what you believe, because what you believe is what you are going to act upon. And what you act upon is what you are going to get. If you don't want to get the wrong thing, you had better act on the right thing. And of course, your acting is based on your believing. If your believing is wrong, your actions will be wrong, and what you receive will be wrong.

James 2:20 tells us, "But wilt thou know, O vain man, that faith without works is dead." Faith without works is dead. Most of the time that passage of Scripture has been used relative to salvation, but the writer is not talking about salvation at all, here. But people have taken that verse to mean that if you are saved, you will act like you are saved. That is a foregone conclusion. But here — he is talking about the operation of the principles of faith. He is saying to you, that if you say you have faith, and you don't have the works to back up the faith, then it is not going to do you any good. In fact, Richard Francis Weymouth's Translation of the New Testament, translates this verse more accurately from the original Greek. Literally, this is what it says: "Faith without corresponding actions will not work on your behalf." That is pretty clear. He is talking about actions that correspond with faith. Now, you can understand why many Christians have not been able to live in victory in many areas of their lives. They have not understood that they have to act upon what they believe (what the Word says). For instance, the Bible says in Matthew 8:17, ". . . Himself took our infirmities, and bare our sicknesses." And in 1 Peter 2:24, we read, ". . . by whose stripes ye were healed." Well, if you were healed, you are, and if you are, you is! That means that you should be well, according to God's Word. Yet think of how many Christians are sick. You can tell why they are sick if you will listen to them talk for three minutes. All they talk about is how sick they are, what is wrong with them, what they have, and how bad they are feeling. They say they believe that they are healed, but they contradict it by their confession. They don't have corresponding actions.

If you believe that you are well, then you are going to have to talk well, act well, and think well, in order for your faith to work for you. You can't believe in healing and then act sick, talk sick, and think sick. You don't have corresponding actions. Your faith is without works, and therefore, your faith is dead.

If I believe I am well, I can't say, "Oh, pray for me. I am so sick. Did I tell you about my latest pain? I have one right here. It just started about five minutes ago."

You can't talk like that and believe that you are well. If you say you believe that you are well, then you ought to talk that, think that, and act like it. If you keep talking like you are sick, keep confessing that you are sick, keep acting like you are sick, you are going to be sick, and there is nothing God can do about it. His Word cannot work on your behalf until you act on the Word.

I found out that with Jesus' stripes, I was not *going to be* healed. He did not say that He was thinking about doing it: He said, "With His stripes ye were healed." I knew that *were* was past tense, not future tense. I knew that if *I were*, or was, *I am*, and if *I am*, **I is**, and **is** is present tense, and that means **NOW!** So I started saying, "I believe I am well." I didn't say that I felt like I was well. I didn't say that I looked like I was well. I didn't say that I understood that I was well. I said, "I believe that I am well." And the reason that I said it, is because the Word said so. I had corresponding actions, and when I had corresponding actions, my faith rose above the sickness, the disease, and the pain, and drove it out. That is the way it works.

You thought you were being honest when you confessed how bad you were feeling. You didn't know that you were being *spiritually dumb*. If you want to be honest, confess what the Word says about you. That is being honest, because whatever God says about you, that's who you are, but you are not going to get the benefits of that until you start saying it.

So — "Faith without corresponding actions is dead." For instance: here is a good sister. She believes she is well. Her physical manifestation has not come yet, so she cannot physically get out of the wheelchair. But she doesn't have to stay in the wheelchair in her spirit. She doesn't have to stay in the wheelchair in her mind. She can see herself well. She can see herself up and around. She can talk, "I believe that I am healed, and I can begin to make plans for the things that I am going to do when I do get out of the wheelchair." But if she just sits there and says, "Oh, I am so sick. I am bound to this chair. I'll never get out, I'll always be like this:" then she will. But she can confess it, if she believes she is well, because that is what the Word says about it.

"Well! That sounds like Science of mind, or *Mind Science*."

No, it is not. It may sound like it, but it is not the same. In *Mind Science*, and metaphysical cults, there are some similarities. They look pretty close to being the same thing, but they are not, because what we are talking about is based on God's Word, and what they are talking about is based on what you have in your head. They say, "It's all a state of mind."

What about all of those people who died from cancer? What did they die of, if there is no such thing as cancer? If it was all in their minds, what was that stuff that ate up their bodies? What was that great big fat thing inside of that woman's stomach that looked like a watermelon, that the doctor said it was a tumor, and was cancerous, and there was nothing they could do when they opened her up? They had to sew her back up, and she died from that thing. How could she die with something that doesn't exist?

Yes, it's real. Sure it's there, but when you walk by faith and the Word of God, instead of confessing with your mouth and seeing with your eyes the things that are in the physical realm, you begin to see the things that are in the realm of God, then you bring God present on the scene. His power will dissolve that cancer, praise God!

Number one: We see then that faith is doing something. And number two: Faith is confessing or saying something. You should confess what the Word of God says about you. If God says you are well, then you must be well. You shouldn't care what your body tells you. You are well because God said that you are. And the Bible says that it is impossible for God to lie (Hebrews 6:18).

Confess this: "If God says with Jesus' stripes I was healed, then I must be healed. I don't care how I feel! I don't care what the doctors say. I don't care what the X-ray machine says! The Word of God says, 'With His stripes, I was healed.' I believe I am well." That might seem foolish to you, but it is according to the Word of God. It is faith with corresponding actions.

I believe that I am well, and I act like a well person would act. Sometimes I do that even in pain. Now, I don't say that I am not hurting, because if I said that I was not hurting, I would be lying about it. I just never talk about how I feel. I only talk about what I believe, and I believe that I am well. When I get my faith moving against that problem of sickness and disease, it drives it right out of my body. Then I begin to walk in divine health, and I don't need healing. Only sick people need healing. Well people don't need healing. You have to get well before you can walk in health.

If you are sick, God has healing available. You can believe His Word and get your healing. Praise God! and go on and live in divine health.

Faith is acting on what you believe. That is the first definition. Remember, what you believe must be based on what is written in the Word. You cannot just dream up some dumb thing like, "Well, I think I will believe that I'll fly like a bird." That won't work. That is *Foolishness*. When you get into faith, faith is acting on what you believe, but what you believe must be based on what is written in the Word.

According to *Webster's Unabridged Dictionary* in common English usage, the word foolishness means "exhibiting folly, deficient in understanding, without judgment or discretion, silly, unwise, stupid, idiotic, senseless, ill-advised, brainless, witless, irrational." Now — when we talk about foolishness, you will know what we are talking about.

Since we are talking about *Faith, Foolishness,* or *Presumption,* we want to find out if our actions are actions of *Faith,* or actions of *Foolishness,* or are our actions merely *Presumption.* Some people cannot tell the difference, and you can tell it by their actions. They have not understood it yet, and they think that they are acting in *Faith,* when they are acting in *Foolishness,* and in some cases, *Presumption.* According to *Webster's Unabridged Dictionary* in use in the English language, *Presumption* means "to take or suppose to be true, or entitled to belief without examination or proof, or on the strength of probability, to take for granted, to infer, to suppose, to assume. That is *Presumption.*

These are the definitions that we will be working with as we continue our study of *Faith, Foolishness, or Presumption.*

2

Owe No Man Anything?

Romans 13:8 says, "Owe no man anything, but to love one another: for he that loveth another hath fulfilled the law." "Owe no man anything . . . ." I believe that this Scripture doesn't necessarily mean that you can't buy something on credit, or buy something on time. The word *owe* in this verse simply means "not being obligated to any man, other than to love him." The only obligation you have to that man is to love that man in God. You don't always have to like the person, but you can love him. You don't have to like him to love him. "Owe no man anything . . . ."

Some Christians have taken the above Scripture to mean this: "I can't buy anything on time or on credit. I shouldn't buy furniture, or a house, or a car, or clothes, or anything on credit." Some will even go so far as to say, "To buy on credit is to use the *world's system*, and that we should not be involved in the *world's system*."

Consider this. You put your money in the bank. You don't bury it in tin cans in your back yard. The banks are a part of the *world's system*. You use banks, don't you? and checks? When you go somewhere you ride in an automobile don't you, or do you still have a donkey pulling a cart behind you? Automobiles are a part of the *world's system*. If you go from one continent to another, you usually go by boat, or by airplane, you don't swim, do you? Well, riding in airplanes is a part of the *world's system*.

"What do you mean by the *world's system?*"

It means *the way the world does it*. If you are not
going to use the *world's system*, you are going to have to
stop wearing clothes, stop getting your hair cut, stop
shaving, stop using electric lights in your house. Electric
lights are a part of the *world's system*. Are you seeing
anything here? It is really ridiculous to say, "I'm not
going to do this, because that's the *world's system*." You
would have to stop doing a whole lot of things. The
difference is this: Christians operate from the undergirding of God's Word, whereas the world operates from the
undergirding of what they can figure out in their heads.
That makes the difference. I can use the same things
that the world uses, but I can use them in the power of
God, and produce the God kind of results. It is the
world's system to plant crops: where do you pull your
crops from? Out of the air? No! We depend on crops too.
We are still operating in the world's system, so just to
say, "the world's system," can be misleading unless you
qualify what you mean by it.

OWE NO MAN ANYTHING . . . .?

When the Scripture says, "Owe no man anything
. . . ." it means, "Don't be under obligation." To be
obligated means that I have agreed to pay something and
I didn't pay it, when I said I would. When I didn't pay it,
then, I really owed it. I am under obligation. Otherwise,
I'm not under any obligation until such time as I agreed
with the man, and the man agreed with me that I pay it.

Let's look at this Scripture verse from another facet.
Think about this: If it is wrong; if it's unscriptural and
unspiritual to buy anything on credit, and to make payments on it, and if that verse in Romans 13:8 really
means that I'm not supposed to buy anything on credit,
then why are there other Scripture passages in the Bible
where God requires you to loan money or goods to some-

body else, and requires them to pay you back? That would be inconsistent. If God doesn't want Christians to owe anything, then it is equally wrong for the sinner to owe anybody. The principle is the same. God's rules are the same. *Up* is *up* to sinners just as it is *up* to Christians, and *down* is *down* to Christians just as it is *down* to sinners.

If this Scripture, "Owe no man anything . . . ." literally means that I'm not supposed to buy anything on credit, and that if I do buy something and make monthly installment payments, I am in violation of the Word, then I shouldn't expect to find any other Scriptures in the Bible where God would encourage me to loan to somebody else. If it is wrong for me to borrow, then it would be wrong for me to lend to someone else, because I would require them to borrow and pay back.

LET'S GO TO THE WORD

Sometimes you have to use one Scripture to clarify another. At face value it may look like, "Owe no man anything . . . ." means "Don't buy anything on credit." I do not believe that this is what God is saying because, if we operated under that premise, we would not be in our building (*Crenshaw Christian Center*), and many people would still be in their sins. Many would still be bound by fear, poverty, sickness, disease, oppression, and depression. But thousands have been made free as a result of coming in contact with this ministry. If we didn't have the building, we wouldn't be here: it wouldn't be *Crenshaw Christian Center*. We didn't have $750,000 to buy this property. That's what they were selling it for —$750,000. We didn't have the cash money, so we are buying it on credit. We have a 15-year mortgage on it, but praise God! it won't take us 15 years to pay it off.

We are going to pay it off before that, but who cares! We are going to have to meet somewhere: Open air, or in some building or enclosure. Do you know anyone who has a building big enough to seat 3,500 people, that will let us use it for free? I doubt it! Well then — we will have to buy our own, and then we can believe God for the money to pay for it, and that is what we have done, and what we are doing. We believe God, and we are paying for it. Praise God, people are being saved, set free, healed, and filled with the Spirit in every service.

I will show you two Scriptures that will help you to understand, because this has really been a stumbling block for many people. For instance, a husband wants to obey the Word, but the kids need clothes, and they sit in their houses on apple crates, because they have no furniture. They have good credit, because they had it before they ever came to Jesus. And they are doing without, when they can have it: as though it were a sin to buy something on credit. Sure, I realize that you have to pay interest on things if you buy them on credit, but you don't really know how much things cost anyhow. They put whatever price tag they want on things. You can go into a store and the price will be marked at $199.95, then there will be a green line marked through that price, and it will be reduced to $159.95; then another line and another tag, special sale marked down to $129.95. Do you think that he is losing money on the item? Not hardly! That joker is not in business to lose money. He is in the business to get you in to buy from him, instead of the man across the street. But all things being equal, the merchant across the street buys from the same manufacturer and pays what everybody else has to pay. Now, some of them are able to buy more at one time so they get a better break on the price. They can afford to sell for less money because they have less overhead, their stores are not as plush, and carpeted.

Consequently, they don't have to put all of their money in furnishings, and they can sell for less.

You can just act like the interest that you pay is a part of what you had to pay for the item, and don't get into bondage over it. There is no point in you sitting around on apple crates, when you can have a nice sofa or couch.

Jesus is speaking here, and He says, "Ye have heard that it hath been said, An eye for an eye, and a tooth for a tooth: But I say unto you, That ye resist not evil: but whosoever shall smite thee on thy right cheek, turn to him the other also. And if any man will sue thee at the law, and take away thy coat, let him have thy cloak also. And whosoever shall compel thee to go a mile, go with him twain. Give to him that asketh thee, and from him that would borrow of thee turn not thou away" (Matthew 5:38-42). It looks as if Jesus is saying that if somebody wants to borrow something from you, you are free to loan it to them, if you want to do so. Whatever he is borrowing from you, he is going to have to pay it back to you. If he says, "Loan me some money; loan me your car; loan me your dog, . . . or whatever," he is borrowing from you. Isn't he? You are lending to him. If it is wrong for you to owe, then why would God tell you to lend to somebody else, and thus cause them to owe you? If owing is wrong, it is wrong for everybody. Whether you know it or not, adultery is not just wrong for Christians: it's wrong for everybody. Fornication is not just wrong for Christians. Nobody is supposed to be committing fornication (sexual intercourse without being married). That is not right for anybody, according to God's Word. If it is wrong for me to owe money, or buy something and make payments on it, it is wrong for me to put another man in bondage to me — to have to owe and pay me. Here, it plainly states: "Give to him that asketh of thee, and from him that would borrow of thee, turn not thou away."

Let's go over into the Old Testament and read from Deuteronomy 28: "And it shall come to pass, if thou shalt hearken diligently unto the voice of the Lord thy God, to observe and to do all his commandments which I command thee this day, that the Lord thy God will set thee on high above all nations of the earth: And all these blessings shall come on thee, and overtake thee, if thou shalt hearken unto the voice of the Lord thy God. Blessed shalt thou be in the city, and blessed shalt thou be in the field. Blessed shall be the fruit of thy body, and the fruit of thy ground, and the fruit of thy cattle, and the increase of thy kine, and the flocks of thy sheep. Blessed shall be thy basket and thy store. Blessed shalt thou be when thou comest in, and blessed shalt thou be when thou goest out. The Lord shall cause thine enemies that rise up against thee to be smitten before thy face: they shall come out against thee one way, and flee before thee seven ways. The Lord shall command the blessing upon thee in thy storehouses, and in all that thou settest thine hand unto; and he shall bless thee in the land which the Lord thy God giveth thee. The Lord shall establish thee an holy people unto himself, as he hath sworn unto thee, if thou shall keep the commandments of the Lord thy God, and walk in his ways. And all the people of the earth shall see that thou art called by the name of the Lord; and they shall be afraid of thee. And the Lord shall make thee plenteous in goods, in the fruit of thy body, and in the fruit of thy cattle, and in the fruit of thy ground, in the land which the Lord sware unto thy fathers to give thee. The Lord shall open unto thee his good treasure, the heaven to give the rain unto thy land in his season, and to bless all the work of thine hand: and *thou shalt lend unto many nations, and thou shalt not borrow"* (Deuteronomy 28:1-12). Here is what I want you to see. The ultimate is to get to the place where you won't have to borrow. That is the goal you should shoot for, so you can get into that position. But you do not start there. Here is the point that I want you to get. He says, "Thou shalt lend unto many nations, and thou shalt not borrow." The reason that you shall not borrow is because you are going to be so blessed that you won't have to borrow. He didn't say that it was wrong for you to borrow. He just said, you won't have to resort to borrowing because you will be the lender, praise God!

If He were saying that you shall not borrow, but that you will lend, then that means that the man who borrows from you is going to owe you. Well, if it is wrong for you to owe, then it is wrong for you to lend to a person, because you will cause him to owe you. Therefore, I don't believe that that verse in Romans 13:8 is saying that it is wrong to buy something on time. I believe that Paul is saying, that the only obligation that I have to my fellow man, or to my brother is to love him.

GROW UP IN YOUR FAITH BY USING IT

If you have good credit and you need a chair in your house, you are one of the King's kids, and there is no point in you sitting on an apple crate: go buy a chair. Then, use your faith to believe for the payments on the chair. When you get your faith developed and it is strong, the next time you need a chair, you won't have to buy it on time. You will be able to pay cash for it. You have to grow, or develop to that point in your faith.

Young married couples, who are just getting started in life, need many things to start their home. Many of them don't have a lot of relatives, or friends who will give them a wedding shower, or reception, and thereby receive many gifts to help them start a home. Most couples don't normally have a whole lot of money, unless they are rich, or well to do, or perhaps, have a rich father. So — if you need something, and you have good credit, go and buy what you need. The important thing to remember is this: Don't look to that method as *the method* for the rest of your life. Only look at it as simply a *means to an end*, and the end being getting into a position where you won't have to buy anything else on time. You have to start somewhere, and that is *Foolishness* — not faith, necessarily to *not buy* something *on time* when you need it. You may not have enough faith to believe for a whole house full of furniture at first. You don't start out with a fully developed and a full grown faith. You have to begin to *use your faith* and *grow up in it*.

Are you going to deprive your child of a baby bed, or your wife of a bed to sleep on instead of a pallet on the floor, just because you want to believe God? It may take you six years before your faith gets to working to the degree where you can go out and buy a house full of furniture. That is *Foolishness* to go without when you can have it if you have good credit and are working on a steady job. It doesn't make sense not to have it.

Now, you can choose to do it (go without), if you want to, but don't make it look as if that is the way that you *have to do it*, in order to be operating in faith. You can buy it on time, and believe God for the payments, and you will still be using your faith. It is a lot easier to pay $75.00 a month on a payment than it is to believe for $2,500 to buy a whole house full of furniture, or a room full — whatever you wish to buy.

I ONCE, WAS IN FINANCIAL ENSLAVEMENT.

Once, we couldn't afford to go out and pay cash for a whole house full of furniture. But the next time we buy some furniture, I am going to pay cash for it! You must remember, I have been using my faith for a number of years. I have my faith in operation. I have faith moving against mountains. I know how to *believe the money in*, now. I paid cash for the last two chairs that I bought for my house; I paid cash for the washing machine, and the last two color televisions, and that was the first time in our lives that we ever paid cash for anything.

Before that, I was doing good to get the credit. They barely let me get the things and make the payments. That's right! Once, I was in such financial enslavement that I couldn't even get credit. I went to a bank and tried to consolidate my debts, and make one monthly payment. That bank refused to loan me any money. "You are a bad risk," they said. "We've been looking at your track record, and we see that you've been getting in debt." Poor things, they didn't realize that the reason I kept getting into debt was because I couldn't get out of owing for the other things. I still needed things: the stove went out; the refrigerator wouldn't work; the chairs broke down; I needed a new table, but I didn't have any extra money, because I was making all of those payments. The only thing that I could do was to either add it on, or borrow. The stores had a limit and they wouldn't add anything to my charge accounts. We were in a terrible state of affairs. We couldn't get any more furniture; couldn't buy anything; we didn't have any money, and because I wasn't making enough money, the bank refused to help me. We had the situation where we had more going out than we had coming in. We lived in that financial bind for years. Sure, I got us into it, and I know it was wrong, but I had signed the papers, and the man had me. There was nothing I could do, except pay for it, or he would come and pick up the stuff, and I would lose it plus all that I had paid on it.

Bless God, I don't need the bank now. It was a struggle, but I found out how to believe God for the payments. I found out how to use my faith, and I began to put my faith to work. We began to believe God on little things, and finally we got our faith moving. We put our faith against the problems of life, and against the financial situations and we believed our way out of every problem, praise God! Now, we can buy almost anything we want and pay cash for it!

"YEAH, BUT WHAT ABOUT PAYING FOR A CAR"?

Is it *Faith*, *Foolishness*, or *Presumption* to buy a car on time?

I have heard people that have heard this faith message say, "Praise the Lord! I am going to believe for a Rolls Royce!" Well, that's fine. King's kids ought to ride around in Rolls Royces. If you have $30,000 to pay down on it, you can have it! You know, that is all it takes: a measly $30,000. Or if you want something sporty: one that everyone else doesn't have, you can buy a Stutz Black Hawk at $50,000. If that is what you desire then you ought to have it. BUT you're going to have to get to the point where you can believe for $50,000. What are you going to do while you are waiting for the $50,000 to materialize? Walk?

If you can't even believe for whatever it costs to ride the bus, how are you going to believe for a $50,000 automobile? No! Praise God. If all you can afford is a Volkswagon, there is no point in you walking in the rain. The King's kids, walking in the rain! Get a Volkswagon, praise God, and start believing God for the payments on it. When you get that Volkswagon paid off, then go buy yourself a Chevrolet, or whatever you want, and believe for the payments on that. Pay that off, and then step up. Finally, you will be believing for a Rolls Royce, if that is what you want.

I would rather have a Lincoln Continental, myself. So whatever it is, different strokes for different folks. The point is, while you are sitting around waiting for the $50,000 to go buy a Stutz Black Hawk, are you going to ride the bus in the meantime, dragging your wife and little kids on the bus, in the rain? Why subject your family to that, when you have good credit? Go buy a car, and then start using your faith and believing God for the payments.

We did that with our car: a 1973 Pontiac. That was the most expensive car we had ever bought in our lives — up until that time. I knew we were in debt, and we didn't have any extra money, but I really didn't know what bad shape we were in. I shall never forget. We came back from a meeting in Tulsa, Oklahoma. As we were flying along, my wife said, "It's just a shame, you are around here, preaching faith, and going to these different meetings, driving an old beat-up Chevrolet." It did look bad. It was dented in on both sides, plus the front and back. So she said, "We're going to buy a car!" I wanted a new car, but I knew we didn't have the money to buy a new car. But I would sure like to drive a new car! It had everything on it that I had ever wanted on a new car. We didn't have to reach over and roll the windows down anymore: just press the button! Hot dog! We were moving up in the world. When we bought that car, we couldn't afford to buy an old ladybug. And those folks tied me up with 42 months of payments, at $155 a month. That was a lot of money.

I didn't know it at the time, but we really didn't have $155 for payments. But you see, we had been using our faith, and my wife had made up her mind that we were going to believe God for the payments on that car. I am here to tell you that that payment was higher than the first trust deed on the house. We believed God for those payments, and that was the easiest thing that we ever paid for in our lives. In fact, we did not have extra money coming out of our regular pay check to cover the payment. We used our faith, and believed God for that money, *over and above our regular pay check*. My wife used her faith and I agreed with her.

All of that time our faith was growing. It was increasing and getting stronger, and stronger as we put it against those issues of life. And finally it got to the point where we were able to believe in — over and above our regular needs, enough money to pay that car off 25 months ahead of time!

Now, that was better than walking around, or riding a bicycle. There was no point in me riding on a bicycle built for two, going somewhere preaching, with my wife on the back and me on the front! So we used our faith and believed for the payments. And through it all, my faith was growing and developing.

As our faith sufficiently developed we paid cash for our next new car, praise God! I would like to point out: if we had started out believing to pay cash for it, we couldn't have even paid for the license tags: that's how much in debt we were. But we started using our faith on making payments, and now that our faith has sufficiently developed—but we haven't arrived yet. We are still on the way up, but we are in the position now, where we can pay cash for almost everything. We have been using our faith for several years now, but in the meantime, why should I have deprived my family of the things they needed?

I have finally come into the position where I now have such a good credit rating, that everybody wants me to get one of their credit cards. They send me letters wanting me to buy this, and buy that, and pay for it any way I want to. Number one: I don't want it. And number two: if I decided to buy it, I would write a check and pay cash for it. But I didn't start out there. It took us seventeen years to get into that debt, and after walking by faith for seven years, we are totally financially independent of the circumstances. How did we get here? We got here by using our faith. We began to use our faith against the small issues of life, and now our faith is in operation to such an extent that we can afford to believe for things and to pay cash for them.

After we believed ourselves into a position of not having to make any monthly payments, the first thing I bought was a second car: I bought my wife a Toyota. It had air conditioning, automatic transmission, radio, heater, tape deck player, and all that! That was what she wanted! And I paid cash for it, praise God! $4,000. That's not bad!

3

Should I Borrow For Life's Necessities?

This is where we live, Friend. As I told you before, we live in a material world. And the primary reason that a man works two jobs is because he doesn't make enough on one job. Don't tell me that a man likes to work that well. If he did he would work *for free*. No. He is trying to get enough money to get ahead. He doesn't realize that the system is geared so that he won't get ahead. The systems of the world, economically speaking, are not designed for you or anybody to get ahead, except for the rich. So the only way that you are going to get ahead is to get rich! And I am on my way.

"Get rich?"

Sure, that's what the Word said. The Word tells us, concerning Jesus Christ, ". . . he was rich, yet for your sakes he became poor that ye through his poverty might be rich " (2 Corinthians 8:9). That's right! But you have to keep things in their proper order. Matthew 6:33 says, "But seek ye first the kingdom of God, and his righteousness; and all these things shall be added unto you." Keep everything in its proper perspective. Don't let things become your goal in life, but simply a means to the end. The kingdom is first. Things are not my goal in life: things are simply stepping stones. Jesus is my goal. My goal is to live in the power of the Spirit of God. These other things just help to make life nicer — that's all.

If the Mafia can ride around in Lincoln Continental town cars, why can't the King's kids? The question is: Is it *Faith, Foolishness, Or Presumption* just because you don't buy a car on time payments, and instead ride on your little bicycle with a tandem car on the side for your wife and three kids to ride in? You are going to believe God for a $50,000 car and you can't even pay for the license on the bicycle. I believe that we established in the last chapter that you need to exercise your faith for the little things, or issues of life, and let your faith grow as you believe God for payments on a smaller car that will be adequate for your family. How is your faith going to grow unless you use it on something? Use your faith on the little issues of life, and it will begin to grow. You don't climb a ladder by starting at the top rung. You start at the bottom and you climb to the top.

I don't want you to get the wrong idea, so I want to emphasize again: I am not saying for you to go out and buy everything on credit and pay interest. I am simply saying, learn to use your faith on the little issues of life (believe for those small payments) until you can become financially independent of the circumstances as your faith grows and develops.

There is a place in Jesus Christ where you can rise above the circumstances economically, and financially. You can be financially independent and financially free, but you're not going to start out like that. Even the Bible tells us to "Grow in grace and in the knowledge of our Lord and Saviour Jesus Christ." That implies that I do not start out with full knowledge, because if I did, I wouldn't have to grow in it. There is a place where we can move in the things of God, when it is faith. But sometimes, we can act presumptuously, or even foolishly.

WHAT ABOUT CREDIT CARDS?

There is nothing wrong in using credit. But it is wrong when you allow credit to use you. I use credit. I have all the credit cards you can name. There was a time when I couldn't even get a credit card. I have been turned down for so many credit cards because my credit rating was bad. They wouldn't even give me a Bankamericard, but praise the Lord, I have them all now. Sure, I use credit cards, but I never pay any charges. This is the most convenient way. I never have to carry $300, or $400 cash in my pocket to buy an airline ticket. I just give them my number.

My checking account is the kind that I have to pay $ .20 each time I write a check. If I go to five stores in one day and make a purchase in each store, I spend $1, just in charges, when I can charge it all on my Mastercharge card and get one bill, and write one check. That's wisdom. I am to the point where I don't have to pay any charges for these credit cards. I use them because of their convenience, and it helps me to keep a better record of my expenses. If I don't use the credit card it will still cost the same amount of money to buy the article, so I *opt* for the card. It keeps my credit established and it makes me look good in the eyes of the world. It opens up a lot of doors that otherwise, I couldn't get into, and then I can become a channel for God's blessing in that situation. I can't become a channel if I can't get in. When the stores have sales the people who have charge accounts get the first notification of the sales, and we are able to take advantage of the sales.

There are many advantages to having credit cards and charge accounts, but I'll not be in bondage to either of them. Any time I sign my name on something, I have the money in the bank to pay for it. It is not a sign of lack of faith to use credit cards. Jesus said, "Be wise as serpents and harmless as doves." Wisdom dictates that it is better to pay $ .20 for one check once a month, than to have to pay $ .20 for each check and end up with $4 or $5 worth of service charges at the end of the month.

Now, I am not telling you to go out and make application for all the credit cards in the world; you may not need them. I use them because I do a lot of traveling in the United States and foreign countries, and it is easier to use credit cards than to try to keep up with the currency exchange rate from day to day. That is a hassle: why fight it? The use of credit cards is international, and most businesses recognize them. There are advantages in using them.

In some situations the use of credit cards and charge accounts may be the better part of wisdom. Thank God, for the little credit those people did let us have, because that was the only thing that kept clothes on our backs. There was a time when that was the only thing that kept us. My kids wouldn't have had any school clothes if it hadn't been for those little measly charge accounts. Every time we would buy two or three things, it would push us over the limit, but at least they could go to school.

Is is *Faith, Foolishness, or Presumption* to use credit? Well, you have to learn how to control yourself, and not let credit control you. Credit can get so easy that you just start buying stuff here and there, and charging and charging, and all of a sudden you get that letter at the end of the month, and boom! you have a $1,000 bill on your hands, and I'll tell you, that will sure knock the wind out of your sails, and that is foolishness.

EBENEEZER SCROOGE OR EBENEEZER PRICE
AT WORK

Who turns away his kids at Christmas? Only Ebeneezer Scrooge, or *Ebeneezer Price*. But we had to do it. Every year we would go out and buy that dumb stuff and charge it, and it would take us all year to pay for it. In the meantime, we would need other things, and I could not buy them, and I would feel guilty, because we were already making payments on our overdrawn accounts. So, we made up our minds that we were not buying anything on credit for Christmas, and we had very meager Christmases for a couple of years. I did this to reach a goal. I didn't even buy a Christmas tree. We didn't need a Christmas tree to throw in the trash after Christmas if it meant going in debt for it. We could use that $20 for something else. Christmas trees do not make Christmas, anyhow.

"Well, what are your kids going to think?"

They are going to think what they want to think anyhow. They are not the ones in debt. They don't know they are riding on a gravy train. I am the one who has to pay the bills. In fact, they are costing me more money. They make the bills; they do not pay them. So, we refused to buy a Christmas tree for a couple of Christmases.

Since that time, we have paid everybody off by using our faith. We now have the most fabulous Christmases ever, and we don't owe anybody anything: hallelujah! That is freedom! But we had to get to that point, and we began by using our faith on the payments. We did not act *foolishly*, and we did not act *presumptuously*, but we acted *in faith*. We took it one step at a time.

WHAT ABOUT A PLACE TO LIVE?

We will look at another aspect. How about a place to live? How about a house? Is it faith to not buy a house and make payments on it? Is that necessarily faith? Are you going to wait until you believe in enough cash to pay for a house, when you aren't doing too well in paying your rent?

You have to stay somewhere, and you only have a few choices. You can stay outside: live somewhere on a vacant lot with nothing over your head. You can get somebody to give you a place to live with no payments involved. And you know how often that happens, don't you? And you can either rent, lease, or buy. Or perhaps, you can stay with relatives or friends, and that can be the worst thing in the world. Those are your basic choices, but you do have to live somewhere.

As I look back on it now, I had in my mind, even in the natural, the kind of house I wanted, before I even learned how to use my faith. I liked architecture, and I used to get architectural drawing books and books of house plans, and I would copy them and landscape them on paper. I was really good at that. I had in mind the kind of house I was going to buy: a ranch style house. I figured that a ranch style house was going to cost me a lot of money. So I was just going to wait until I got the money, and then buy the house. All of that time, (stupid, ignorant *me*) I was paying rent, and getting nothing for it. We paid rent for ten years, and when those ten years were up we left that apartment with only the clothes on our backs. We had made the landlord rich, and we still didn't have a thing.

Renting — as far as I am concerned is like taking your money into the bathroom, putting it in the toilet, and flushing it. That is how much you get for your money. Actually, buying a house is an investment. Buying a house is using wisdom. You are going to have to live somewhere. So if you are going to pay rent, why not believe God for the payment on a house? Every time you make that payment, you are paying yourself something. When you rent, every time you pay the rent, you are paying that man something. And you get nothing back. That's right.

Just to show you how this can work, I am going to share an experience with you. We bought a house that cost $12,500 in an area where it wasn't really my choice to live. But an opportunity opened up, and we were able to get this house some years ago for $500 down. At that time, getting $500 together was like pulling eye teeth. We finally scrounged and scrounged, and with the help of a broker who was a relative, we finally got the down payment on the little house, and we made payments on it for 3½ years. We were in such bad shape financially, that we couldn't even put any paint on that house, on the outside. We finally were able to paint the inside, and we fixed it up so it was really nice. Then one day I said, "We need to move to the other side of town;" and we decided to sell the house. We were pastoring on the other side of town, and I was working in Culver City, which was just about two miles from the church, and I was driving from Culver City to home, which was about twenty miles one way, and from home all the way back, almost to the same place, to the church, two or three times a week; I was driving myself *buggy*.

Although we didn't know much about selling a house, or even if we could get anything for our equity, we sold that house that we bought for $12,500 for $16,950, and that gave us $5,000 to put down on another house. Now that is wisdom. We paid the loan off and got more cash out of that house than we had put into it.

Remember, we wouldn't have had anything if we had been renting for that 3½ years.

As I said before, you are going to have to live somewhere. And I believe if you have the opportunity to get a house, get it. You are going to either believe for house payments or rent. And the prices they are charging for rent now is absolutely outrageous. I have listened to people talking about their rental payments and my payment on my house was nothing compared to the rent that they were paying. And they didn't even have any privacy. They had to put up with those idiots next door, throwing their parties all night long, banging on the wall, and doing all that other stuff.

You can get your own vine and fig tree: your own house, praise God! Your kids can run free. If they want to pull the flowers off, they can do so. Nobody is going to cut their heads off. In an apartment you can't walk on the grass, you can't touch the plants, you can't do this, that, or the other. In a lot of places, they will not even rent to people who have children.

You have to believe God for rent. Get your faith working, and believe God for the down payment on the house, and payments on the house. Don't try to move up on the hill into a $100,000 house the first time you exercise your faith. What I am pointing out is, if you live in an apartment, you can live in a house. And in the meantime, keep making those payments, and paying that money to yourself. That is on your account now, and not to the landlord's. You are putting that in for yourself. Get your faith working, and you will get to the place where we are in our lives. By making the payments, and using our faith on the payments, we got to the point where we could pay the house off *20 years ahead of time*. We don't owe anybody anything on our house. Now, we have a good investment that we are sitting on, that we can parley into another house. I am going to buy another house. We need a larger house, and I want to move closer to the church. I want to have more of the church people in our home, and to have the opportunity to have more fellowship with them. We need room for that. In fact, we already believe that we have a larger home. Our plan is to pay cash for the next house.

Now, I couldn't do that a few years ago. I was barely making the payment on the house. But I started using my faith.

Foolishness would be to sit around and try to wait and believe for a $150,000 house. It takes more faith force to believe for $150,000 than for $150. Why do that? Believe for $150 a month — believe for your rent, or the payment on the first trust deed on the house, and then all the time, you are putting money in the bank for yourself. As I have said, you have to live somewhere, and if you have good credit take advantage of it. Use your credit, but don't let it use you, and I believe that God will bless you.

Is isn't necessarily *faith*, because you sit at home on your apple crates in your living room with no carpet on the floor, and no furniture in the house. No pictures on the wall, with your Bunsen burner in the kitchen to cook your food on because you don't have a stove, and eating on paper plates because you can't afford to buy china. Get a house, and believe God for the payments, and get your faith to moving. It is a lot easier to believe for $150 a month than it is to believe for $100,000. It doesn't take as much faith force. But as you keep on believing you are going to be strengthening your faith muscle. As you strengthen that muscle, you will be able to pick up heavier loads. And soon, you will be able to believe for a

$100,000 house, and pay cash for it. I believe *that is faith*. I believe that it is *foolishness* just to sit around and do nothing. Now, different strokes for different folks. You do what you want. I'm free, so whatever you do doesn't affect me. I am telling you how you can get free. It works!

"Well, God did that for you because you are a preacher."

Oh, come on. I don't want to hear that. I can take you all over the city of Los Angeles, and show you preachers who don't even have a church to preach in. They preach in store fronts, and can't even pay the rent on that. You don't get blessed because you are a preacher. You get blessed because you operate in line with the Word, according to faith. That is how you get blessed. I don't care if you are black or white, brown or yellow, green or red-polka-dotted, educated, or uneducated, you are not going to get blessed because of that. God is only going to confirm His Word, with signs following. Why didn't God bless me the first seventeen years that I was a preacher? I was poor and struggling: I didn't have anything. I hated to face another day: it was agony. I didn't know where the money was coming from. But I was still a preacher, and I wasn't being blessed.

I HAD TO ACT IN LINE WITH THE WORD OF GOD

I started getting blessed when I started doing what God's Word told me to do. When I began to use my faith instead of operating in *foolishness*, and I began to act in line with the Word of God instead of *presumption*, then that put God to work on my behalf. The power of God came into play and God moved things out of the way. As I moved in faith, God honored it, because He confirms His Word with signs following. Praise the Lord! It works, but you are going to have to work it. So — get out of that bag that you are in, and move in *faith*.

If you are a young husband, and you are marrying a girl and taking her into an empty bedroom, and calling that "home," that isn't faith (necessarily). Start using your faith and believe God to go ahead and get a house, and buy some furniture. Use wisdom, and don't over-extend yourself. Don't do as I did: make $100 a week and have to pay out $115 a week in bills. That won't work. You will be in trouble that way.

You have the Spirit of God in you to give you wisdom. Don't buy beyond your ability to pay. Use your faith on those payments and make the payments on the furniture, and house: believe God every time you make a payment. Believe God for an excess to come in, over and above that, so you can pay the thing off, and you will soon get to the point where you can pay cash for everything else you want. There is nothing in the world that feels so good, as to be able to walk into a store and tell the salesman, "I want one, and I want that one in green, and I want that one." And when they ask you how you are going to pay, charge or cash? You can say, "Cash, man. Cash!" That is faith, and I tell you it makes life beautiful when you operate that way. So don't think it's faith, just because you are sitting around doing nothing: that may be foolishness.

It may be presumptuous for you to attempt to believe for a $100,000 house when you don't have enough faith to believe for $150 a month rental payment. When you move up to a $100,000 house, you will end up paying $2,000 or $3,000 a year for taxes. And if you stop and think about it, that is much more than $150 a month that you are making in payments. How are you going to come up at the end of the year with $3,000 for taxes? The higher you go, the more it will cost you to be up there. The bigger the car, the more the license tags. Everything goes up correspondingly. When you buy $300 suits, you can't wear a $1.95 tie: that just won't work. You will end up getting into silk ties at $12.50, up.

You must start right where you are, and begin to use your faith. The more you become free, the freer Jesus is in you, to flow out of you and the greater impact you can have on the environment around you. Then they will see your joy: they will see your peace: they will see your victory, and they will see you overcoming every circumstance and situation. They will want to know, "Who is your source?"

You will tell them, "Jesus is the One who puts me over and puts me on top: Praise God!"

That is the way it works. It works! Oh, let me tell you it works! If you are not working it, I feel for you. It works, but it is only going to work in context with God's Word. So begin to use your faith for the little things, and pretty soon, you will get to that point where you will begin to believe for more and more. And this is the most exciting part of all. You will get to the point where you will be able to believe for somebody else's needs. That is when it really starts getting good. It works, praise the Lord.

4

Stepping Stones In The Faith Walk

I believe that we have adequately shown that when the Scripture says in Romans 13:8, ". . . Owe no man anything . . . ." it does not necessarily mean that you cannot buy something on time, and make installment payments on it. You don't look to that as the end, or the way it should be for the rest of your life, but you think of it in terms of getting out of debt. You use it as a *stepping stone*, because the faith life is a progressive development in faith. Nobody is born a full grown physical adult. They are not born fully developed, mentally, physically, and psychologically. Some of us have gotten into a bag of thinking that just because a person is born again, they are born again a fully developed Christian, but they are not. They are born babies, and because they are babies, they have to grow up. Sometimes, they try to act like they are grown-up spiritually, when in fact, they are not, and it won't work.

I am sure that a six year old child can see an automobile or fire truck as it passes by, but I doubt if he is thinking that he can drive them. He might try it. He might climb upon the seat, but his little feet wouldn't even touch the floor boards. He couldn't drive either of them if he wanted to. He can't even put his foot on the accelerator pedal. He is not big enough physically. It is the same with some people who have heard the faith message. They can hear about the fact that they don't have to be sick, and they don't have to be poor, and they can desire that and want it, but their faith life — their spiritual life — is not sufficiently developed to handle it.

And they go off and say, "I am not going to go to the doctor any more. I am not going to use medicine any more:" and they do not have their faith sufficiently developed to believe for a broken finger nail: and they are trying to believe for deliverance from cancer. It won't work. That is not *faith*, that is *foolishness*.

Use the means that are available to you as stepping stones to get to that point where you won't have to use stepping stones any more. When you first start out, you are not there yet. You do not start out at the end: you start out at the beginning. Many people are acting very foolishly, and they are not acting in faith at all.

CAN'T I JUST BELIEVE GOD FOR LOTS OF MONEY?

Let's look at another aspect in our everyday life relative to *faith*. This is an area where people can get bogged down. They want to know about believing God for money. I run into people all of the time, who want to start right out believing God for a million dollars. Some people think that God will cause it to come to them just because they think about it. *He will* cause a million dollars to come to you, *if* you have your faith sufficiently developed to believe for it.

If you haven't been doing too well believing for quarters, what makes you think that you are going to believe for a million dollars? It takes more *faith force* to believe in a million dollars, than it does to believe for a quarter.

FAITH IS A FORCE

Think with me about *faith*. Aside from all the definitions that we have given you, think of *faith* as a *force*. It really is. *Faith is a force*. It has power inherent within it. If you will think of faith as a force, you will realize that it can be developed in ability to push or move an object.

I fly a lot, as I travel from one place to another. And the power of the modern day jet aircraft never ceases to amaze me, especially when I am riding on the "big birds," like the L1011's, DC10's, or 747's. The pilot does not taxi out to the take-off runway, press a button, and zip that plane is in the air, flying, with the wheels up. NO. He has to start out slowly on that runway, and you can hear the whine of the engines as he pushes the throttles forward. The plane begins to move, slowly at first, then faster and faster, as he continues to push the throttles fully open, and until the plane is moving fast enough to become airborne. But he doesn't start off at his takeoff speed of 125-130 miles per hour. He starts at zero, and works up to that. If you could just think of your faith that way. The engines can't push the plane into the sky all at once. It is the same with faith. You have to build up and develop your faith force in your life, and then put it against the issues of life. Don't try to put your faith force against an issue when you don't have that force developed to push that issue, because you will be operating in *presumption*, and in *foolishness*.

It is not a matter of God not wanting you to have a certain thing. It may be that your faith is not sufficiently developed to handle it. You faith force is not strong enough to move or push that object into existence. You can take one of these little private planes like a Piper Cub or a Cessna, or something like that, and you could put it in behind one of those giant 747's and try to push it down the runway, but it won't work. That little plane could never push it down the runway. It doesn't have the power. You have to have a lot of power in operation to push that much weight. Your faith is like that. It is a real force, but it has to be developed. As you get it into motion, and keep it moving, you can push greater and greater objects: whether it be an object of debt, or sickness, or whatever, you develop your faith. Don't try to start out from the take off runway, and just jump into the sky and be airborne. You can't do it. Airplanes can't do it and neither can you.

Everywhere I go, I don't care what color the people are, or what plateau of life they are living on, how well educated they are, you can hear the same cry coming from the mouths of everybody. "What about money? I don't have enough money. How can I get some more of it? What about believing God for finances?"

Some people hear this *faith message* and they go out and quit their jobs. I have actually known people who have gone out and quit their jobs. "Oh, praise God, Brother Price, I am going to live by faith." You can see right there that they have missed the whole thing. They think that living by faith means to live without any visible means of support. That is not living by faith, and that is how the Word of faith has received such a bad connotation in the minds of many people.

Usually the people who say, "I am going to live by faith;" and they go out and quit their jobs, have a wife and a baby, and they don't have food on the table. Yet they call that "living by faith." They say, "We are going to believe God, Brother Price. The Lord is going to provide."

Provide what? Quitting your job is not living by *faith*. Not only is it *foolishness*, but it borders on presumption. You don't have any Scripture upon which to support that kind of action.

"Well, I am going to believe God. I am not going to work."

Not working is not necessarily an act of faith. It could be an act of laziness. It doesn't automatically mean faith. God is going to work through channels. And I have said this before, and I shall say it again: God is not going to drop any money out of the sky on you. If you are sitting around waiting for God to drop $1,000 out of the sky on you, you are going to be waiting a long time. God doesn't operate like that. God is going to bring what He brings to you through some man. Even if you walk down the street and find some money, it came through some man.

"Brother Price, God will just make some money. God can do anything."

No He can't! He can't do everything. He can't lie. The Bible says that it is impossible for God to lie, so that is something He can't do. He can't save you unless you come in repentance. You won't get saved unless you come in repentance, and believe in Jesus. The Bible says that "God is not the author of confusion," so He can never start an argument. If there is an argument, God is not in it. He did not start it. You see — there are some things that He cannot do. Neither can God pour money out of the sky on us. If He did, He would be a counterfeiter.

"Well," you say, "I don't understand that!"

Sure you do. The United States Treasury Department has already issued all the currency for the United States. It is all in serial numbers, in sequence. Anybody else that introduces any other money into this economy is branded a counterfeiter, and if you don't believe it, you go make you some money, and start spending that money and see how long you last. They will put you behind bars as a counterfeiter. All the money is already in circulation. God can't just create some money. If He did, what serial numbers would they have on them? Those $100 bills that you say that God will create, what serial numbers would they have on them, and what sequence would they fall under? As soon as the Treasury Agent looks at the numbers and sees that there are no serial numbers on them, you are really in trouble. How is God going to do it?

I used to have that dream-state idea: that somehow, God would just reach out over the balcony of heaven, and yell, "Hey, Fred," and drop it down.

And I would just run out and say, "Ah-ha! Got it!" It doesn't work that way. That is *foolishness;* that is not *faith.* God is going to work through the hands of men. He will move on the hearts of men. He can work through a job.

You may pray and say, "Lord, I need $100;" and you thought that the $100 was just going to materialize out of nowhere. No. It may come in the form of a job. It may come in the form of overtime that nobody else can get but you. It may come in the form of a raise, or it may come in the form of something else coming to you that you didn't even expect to get. Don't think that because you walk by faith, you do not work. That is *presumption*, and you have no Scripture on which to stand.

IF YOU DON'T WORK, YOU SHOULDN'T EAT

Paul gives us something in 2 Thessalonians 3:10-15, that may be a *mind boggler* for some who read this book. Notice — Paul didn't say this to us, "If you can work it into your busy schedule, or see if it will fit into your denominational doctrine . . . ." No! He said, "For even when we were with you, this we commanded you, that if any would not work, neither should he eat. For we hear that there are some which walk among you disorderly, working not at all, but are busybodies" (vv. 10,11). Times haven't changed, have they? "Now them that are such we command and exhort by our Lord Jesus Christ, that with quietness they work, and eat their own bread" (v. 12). In other words, not sponging off the neighbors: not sponging off their other brothers and sisters in Christ, under the guise of "I'm believing God for mine. My ship will come in some day." Your ship has sunk, Baby. You had better get yourself a job. Your ship is under the water. The Book says that every man ought to eat his own bread. "But ye, brethren, be not weary in well doing. And if any man obey not our word by this epistle, note that man, and have no company with him, that he may be ashamed. Yet count him not as an enemy, but admonish him as a brother" (vv. 13—15). Now, that is very plain, isn't it? Yet a lot of people hear this faith message and they think that they are going to just run out and believe God.

You can believe God through your job. God will work through your job. Perhaps you have had opportunities, and you prayed and believed God, and you thought that the money was just going to fall out of the sky, and somebody said to you, "Do you want to do some extra work?"

"No, not me, I believe in God, Brother. I ain't got no time for no work. Don't you see, my hands are clean. I believe in God."

That is not believing in God. You are operating in *foolishness*. God may bring you the job, a job that nobody else can get, at a time when nobody else can get it, and have them paying you money that nobody else could get. That will be God providing. He works through channels. It is *foolishness* and *presumption* to think that you are going to exist without working.

"Well, Brother Price, you don't work!"

That is the dumbest thing you ever said. The ministry is work. It is my job. The Scripture says, "Muzzle not the ox, that treadeth out the corn:" and, "They that preach the gospel should live of the gospel." That means that when a man is in the full-time ministry, that ministry ought to support him, and pay all of his bills, and if it doesn't, he ought to get a job! The ministry may look like play to you, but it is work. It is my job. It is the job the Lord has given to me, and as I am faithful in it, He always provides all my needs. Because I am operating by faith doesn't mean that I can sit around and do nothing. If I do, I am going to be like the ones who won't work: they have nothing, they sit in a bare house with nothing on the floor, and they sit on apple crates, and the baby has to sleep in a box, when they could get out and get themselves a job.

If you are sitting around saying, "I am waiting on the Lord, the Lord is going to supply my needs;" you are just lazy, that's all. The Bible is very plain about the fact, that if you do not work, you should not eat.

"I believe in God, Brother Price."

What are you believing for?

"I believe in God to supply my needs."

What do you think that was when that man walked up to you and offered you that job for $250 a week? Your finances may come through a job. It may come through opportunities. I have had opportunities to go places, and minister when it looked like a hopeless case, and a waste of time to go. But I was obedient to God, and I went. I didn't expect to get anything. In fact, I expected to pay my own way. I figured the situation was so poor just looking at it, but God spoke to the people, and the blessings just came out of the walls. Folks would walk up to me and say, "The Lord told me to give you this," and I received many times more than I even dared to expect.

God will work through the situations. Somebody might give you a back yard to clean up. Living by faith does not mean that you don't have a job. Living by faith means that you do not *look to that job* as the source of your supply, but only as one of the available channels that God is using to pipe the money to you. There is a big difference. Please notice what I said: The man who walks by faith does not look to the job as the source of his supply, but simply as a present available channel that God is using. God is my source, but it may be your hand that is the channel. It may be the job that might be the channel, but I don't look to the job as my source. You can easily tell the difference between the man who walks, or lives by faith, and the man who is looking to the job as the source of his supply. When they start talking "layoff," the man who looks to his job as his source, starts getting a jumpy stomach. He starts losing sleep; he starts getting cold, sweaty hands, every time he hears the telephone ring, or the intercom from the big boss' office he starts shaking in his boots, and perspiration breaks out on him. His source begins and ends with the job. When you talk "layoff," he runs scared, because his source is about to dry up.

The man who lives by faith is not worried about the economic situation. The man who walks by faith is not worried about the cost of living going up. Suppose eggs go up to $5 a dozen. Suppose gas goes up to $10 a gallon. What is that to our Heavenly Father? He owns the cattle on a thousand hills. He has a city up there with streets paved with gold. That's no big thing. The man who lives by faith is not concerned.

Sometimes, even now, as we are being so blessed, I have to help my wife along. She came out of a kind of poverty thinking situation. Every once in awhile, she gets a little disturbed about how high the price of meat is, and the high price of coffee. And I say, "So what? Who cares how high it is? Honey, we can afford it! Our Father is rich in houses and lands, and we are not going to deprive ourselves of the niceties of life, and the necessary things, and the things we even want, because we don't have the money. We believe we do have the money, and God will get that money to us because we are looking to Him as our source of supply." The things in the natural don't cause us to run scared. The man who walks by looking at his job as the source of his supply, runs scared when you start talking about price hikes, and tax rises. Who cares? Taxes may go up, I don't want them to, but my Father can afford it.

God is our source. When you talk about faith and finances, and believing God for money, you had better wake up and realize that money may come to you through a job. He will open up a way for you to make it. Suppose the job only lasts a week? So what? He is not the God of just one week. He is the God of all weeks. And He will have another job at the end of that week.

LIVING BY FAITH DOESN'T MEAN QUITTING YOUR JOB

Don't think that because you are walking by faith, you are supposed to run out there and quit your job. If you have done so, and you are talking about how you are believing God, you are acting in *presumption*, and you have no Scriptural basis to stand on. Let's read these words again, that Paul gave to us, through the anointing of the Holy Spirit. "For even when we were with you, this we commanded you, that if any would not work, neither should he eat" (2 Thessalonians 3:10).

Wife, if that rascal is not working, don't feed him any more. Tell him to go get himself a job. Tell him that when he goes and gets himself a job, you will cook for him. I believe that you can help that rascal to get off of his *rusty dusty* if you stop cooking for him, and he will get out and work. A lot of people say, "Bless God, Brother Price, I have to give time to the Word. I have to study the Word." You are studying the Word while your kids are starving to death? That is not *faith*. That is *presumption*. That is *foolishness*. "But I have to get alone with the Lord." You had better get alone with the employer so that you can get alone with your pay check at the end of the week. There is plenty of time at the end of the day for you to get alone with the Word, and get alone with God. The Bible is telling you that you had better work. And if you are not working, you should not eat. So, the next time that *job quitter* comes home and says, "Where is my dinner?" tell him that if he doesn't work, then he doesn't eat. You have the Bible to back you up. The Scripture is right there. Let him get mad at God if he wants to, but this is where we live. Too much of what is called "faith," is foolish thinking. You have quit your job, and you call that "believing God?" as you stand out there and wait for the ravens to bring you bread and flesh in the morning, and bread and flesh in the evening.

"Yeah, but that's what God did for Elijah."

Is your name Elijah?

"No!"

Well, you had better stop looking for the ravens then. That is not *faith*, that is *presumption* and *foolishness*.

Work! God will operate through that job. I can give you testimony after testimony of people who have worked on their jobs, believed God, and God has raised them up, given them raises, bonuses, and things they did not expect to get, and He has just blessed them in every way possible through that channel. When that channel becomes too small for God to get to you what He wants you to have, He will move you out of there. He will move you to another position, move you to another company. Who cares what company it is? He will bless you through that channel, as you walk in faith, believing.

It is foolish, talking about how you are going to believe God, and not going to work. You don't have any Scripture to stand on. That is *presumption* — not *faith*. God will provide your finances through any channel that you have open. Your job is one channel.

5

Insurance? To Have Or Not To Have

Another area which seems to be a stumbling block to many Christians is the question of insurance. Some people have the idea that to walk by faith means that you shouldn't have any insurance: no automobile insurance, no fire insurance, no life insurance, and no medical insurance.

Is that walking by faith? Is that what faith means? I know some who teach that.

I believe that it is wrong to tell another person to get rid of his or her insurance, because that puts people into bondage. If you teach this, you do not know that person's *level of faith*. Maybe you can do it, and if you wish to do so, that is fine, but don't impose that on other people, and make it mandatory for everyone, because you have no Scriptures to stand on. If you choose to get rid of all your fire insurance, and your life insurance, and your medical plan, health plan, and your automobile insurance, that is wonderful! If you want to do it, but you cannot make that a mandatory proposition for everybody else, because you have no idea where somebody else's faith is.

Anybody with two ounces of sense knows that insurance does not keep things from happening. Fire insurance does not stop fires. Medical insurance does not stop sickness, does it?

"No."

Well, what about insurance? To have or not to have it? That is the question.

Many of you readers, have had an automobile, and
have had automobile insurance: collision, liability,
whatever, and still have had an accident. I am sure that
you did not intend to have that wreck. But you had that
wreck because, *number one:* you are imperfect: *number
two:* you live in an imperfect world: *number three:* your
environment is imperfect, and *number four:* those other
nuts driving on the street are imperfect, just like you. So
the insurance does not stop the accident from happening.
We are talking about automobile insurance not stopping
an accident from happening. But I will tell you what it
can do: It can stop the devil from taking everything you
own. You know the Bible tells us in Ephesians 4:27,
"Neither give place to the devil." It is saying, "Don't
give the devil any place." The word *place* in the Greek is
the word *Topos*, and it is the word which we derive the
English word *topography. Topography* has to do with the
contour and the surface of the land: islands, mountains,
valleys, in other words, the shape of the land. What the
Bible is saying is, "Don't give the devil a rock to stand
on. Don't give him an inlet, a peninsula, a cape, an
island, a mountain peak, a valley: don't give the devil
any place."

Think about this; especially relative to automobiles
in the United States of America. What is the one thing
that an individual wants to do as soon as you hit him?
Especially, if you hit him from behind? The first thing
that he wants to do is sue you. And he doesn't want to
sue you for just the $10 or so that it takes to get an
X-ray picture. He doesn't want to sue you just for the
$15 that he will pay for the consultation with the doctor.
He doesn't want to sue you just for the $50 he loses for
not being able to go to work. He wants to sue you for
$1,000,000. Why? Because in this society, people are so

money hungry that they will take everything away from you if they can, and feel nothing about it.

As a Christian, you know that you are not looking to the insurance to keep you from having a wreck, because if you are, you are going to miss it, but that is one place that you can stop the devil, and he will never be able to take anything away from you.

I'm sure that you think you are a good driver. I consider myself a very good driver, but I have done some things that I could not help. I didn't intend to do it, but I did it. Why? Because I am imperfect.

To give you an illustration. We had a Toyota, and Cheryl, my daughter (she was eighteen at this time) was on her way to school one day and had an accident. I don't know what happened because I wasn't there. Cheryl didn't really know what happened either, it happened so fast. One thing that she knew was she hit the car in front of her, and the car in front of her hit the car in front of him, and the lady behind Cheryl's car hit her: that was all that she knew. When she looked up, everybody's car was in perfect condition, because they were big cars, but the front end of her Toyota was smashed all the way back to the front doors. The first thing that the man in front of her wanted to do (He didn't have a scratch on his car, not even a scratch on his bumper.) was sue. Sure, I commission the angels to watch over my kids. Nothing can happen to them physically to permanently hurt them. But they may do some dumb thing, and if they do some dumb thing, they are going to get in a dumb wreck. Remember, you are not perfect, and though your intentions are not to get in a wreck, you are in an imperfect situation.

If you are the head of your household, I am talking primarily to you. You may be a single woman, a single man, a husband, whatever. You may be a divorced woman who does not have a husband, but you do have children: you have a responsibility to do whatever you can to protect your family. Stop and think about it: insurance is not against God. They don't issue insurance against God in that sense. They are trying to help you. I have automobile insurance, but I am not looking to that automibile insurance as the source of my protection. I have the minimum amount of automobile insurance that the law requires me to have. I could go out and buy $5,000,000 worth of automobile insurance to keep me from having an accident. But I have a wife and two daughters living with me. The youngest is not ready to drive yet, but she is going to drive, and she is probably going to have her whack at it when she gets there. I am not making a negative confession. I am talking facts. I did not talk that child into wrecking that car, but when I got home, it was wrecked. It was wrecked to the tune of $700. I have better things to do with my money than to pay somebody to fix up dented fenders. I didn't even dent it. I wouldn't have minded it so much if I had dented it, but I wasn't even driving the car! You know, that gets to you: paying for someone else's mess up. But she is my child. She didn't ask to come here. I brought her into the world, and I have to do all within my power that is reasonable to protect her in every way.

Why?

Because there is a ruthless society out there, and a ruthless devil, and a pack of ruthless demons that will try to kill them any way they can.

I know she did not want to have the wreck anymore than she intended to have it, because she didn't want to face me. Don't you feel bad when you have wrecked something that belongs to someone else? You don't want to face them. Cheryl and Stephanie were both in the car, and neither got a scratch. It could have been worse! I have seen people get killed and there wouldn't be a scratch on the car. But I have the angels watching over them. Yet, the angels can only protect you to the extent that you obey the existing laws. I don't mean just the law of 35 mph., but the laws that operate in the physical world. When you violate those laws, you are going to pay some consequences. I don't care if you talk in tongues. You are going to pay some consequences, and anything that can minimize the consequences, I am all for it. Anybody can mess up, you know.

WHAT ABOUT HEALTH INSURANCE?

I am not going to spend all of my money on insurances, and go out and buy $50,000 worth of life insurance. I don't need that! But I do have some minimum things to protect my family. Let's talk about health insurance. Some of these young men are getting married, and they have come into contact with the Word of Faith, and they have decided that they are not going to buy on time, or have any insurance, and they are not even going to go to the doctor. I believe that that is a marvelous goal to shoot for. I am shooting for it myself on a minute-by-minute, second-by-second basis. But I have not arrived there yet. I am not perfect yet, and neither are you.

Suppose your wife's female organs are giving her such a fit, she just doesn't want to stand against any more pain. You are the husband, you are the provider, and she is of age, and maybe she has heard the Word, but your faith cannot override her faith. She has to at least be in agreement with you. You cannot override her will. Suppose she says, "I don't want to go through another one of these natural childbirths. I want you to take me to the doctor, and let him give me a shot and put me to sleep. I don't want any more of that pain."

What are you going to do? Tell her, "No. You are going to have a natural childbirth, or go to hell." Of course not. Some would think so. Stop and think about it Doctors are not opposed to divine healing. They are not opposed to God.

I do everything as accurate as I can, but I am not perfect. I can guarantee you this, I am always shooting for perfection. I want to be perfect before God. I don't consider myself perfect, but I am sure trying. Let me tell you about an incident that happened to me.

One night, it was very late, we were coming from a 24-hour market and I did something real dumb. I didn't mean to do it, but I did it. I was very familiar with the area, although I will have to admit that the direction in which I was driving at that time was not one that I drove very often. Since it was very late at night, there were no cars on the street. Now, I am a law abiding citizen. It is always my intention to obey the law. We came to this signal, and I wanted to make a left turn, and as we approached the intersection, I suddenly realized that I was not in the left-turn-lane. I glanced up at the signal, and I saw green, so I whipped over into the left turn lane, and made my turn, Right in the middle of the turn, I suddenly realized that the left turn lane was controlled by a separate signal. I thought I saw something red back there when I saw the green. And I looked back quickly, and realized the green light was for the through traffic, and the red for the left turn lane. What was I going to do? I was wrong. I didn't intend to do it. I was sincere. God knew that I didn't mean to make that turn like that. I wouldn't have disobeyed the law for anything in the world. You could not get me to go through, but I did it. Thank God, there were almost no cars on the street at that hour of the night. But that could have happened at any intersection. But "Holier than Thou. Perfect me!" I did it!

The point I am trying to make is you need to realize your wife is not perfect. Your kids are not perfect, and you, as a father, as a husband, and as the head of the house, have the responsibility to provide for and protect your family to the best of your ability. Yes, pray for them. Sure, put the angels around them. But I say, use anything that is available to you to stop the enemy that's not in conflict with God's Word. After all, I can't find anywhere in the Bible where it says, "Don't go to the doctor. Don't have insurance, and don't wear seatbelts, or use a parachute."

PAUL DIDN'T STOP A STORM

If you will look at the latter part of the book of Acts, you will find the great Apostle Paul, who had several visions of the Lord Jesus Christ, and wrote more than half of the New Testament, was on board a ship, and they lost everything on that ship.

"Why didn't Paul stop the storm?"

I don't know. Jesus did, but Paul didn't. But nobody's life was lost. They lost the ship, they lost the cargo, they lost everything on board that ship. In fact, an angel appeared to Paul and said, "No loss of life shall be sustained, if everybody stays on board the ship."

"Well, why didn't God stop the storm? Why didn't Paul stop the storm? Why lose all that cargo?"

There were over 200 people on that ship, and nobody's life was lost. That is the most important thing. What is a car? Nothing but a piece of metal. What is a house? Some plaster, and electrical wires. You can get another house, but you can't get another you!

I can't get any more children like the ones I have now. I can't get another wife like the one I have now. And I have an obligation to protect them. Yes, I am praying for them. Yes, I have the angels encamped around them. Yes, I set the angels around Cheryl that day she went to school, but she still had the wreck. If I had not had the insurance, that joker would have tried to sue me, and I would have had to put up a lot more faith to fight him off with all the demons that were behind him, trying to sue me to get rich. On top of that, I would have had to shell out $700 for nothing. So, thank God, I had insurance. It kept the devil off my back. You see, I am covered. I have all the proper insurance that I should have, and I am not going to spend any money for any more. I am not going to give the devil a place in me. He is not going to take everything from me over some dumb automobile accident.

You can govern yourself accordingly. I am not going to tell you to get insurance, or not to get it. But I think you do need to stop and think; if you have responsibilities to somebody else, you owe them something.

Most reputable doctors are doing everything they can to help you sustain your life, are they not? Medicine is not against divine healing. Medicine tries to get you well. Well, I believe that there is a place in God where you can come to, in your own individual life, where you won't need a doctor, or the medication. But you have a family, you have a wife, you have kids. You have a responsibility to them. Many times, a man is talking about faith, and it is not faith at all. It is foolishness, or presumption. Sometimes, he is plain stingy. He doesn't want to pay the premiums. Then he is going to insist that his wife believes. But suppose his wife doesn't believe? Suppose this time, she is just tired of standing against the pain, and she says, "Take me to the doctor?"

What are you going to do? Tell her, "Well, Honey, believe for your healing or die?" Are you going to tell her that, when it is within your power to help. You know as well as I do, if you have any sense at all, that doctors cannot heal. You are not looking to the doctor as your healing source. You know that healing comes from God, but until the healing physically manifests itself, what about that pain?

If you are hurting, why should you stay awake all night long with pain pills right next to your bed? All you have to do is take that pill and get a good night's sleep. Now, understand what we are talking about. We are talking about *Faith, Foolishness, Or Presumption*. I am not saying to get you a bunch of pills and lean on them.

I don't use pills myself, because I do not need them, but if I needed one, I would take it, and not feel a thing about it. I have my faith operating to such an extent that I just don't need them. That doesn't mean that I don't get attacked, but I am willing to take whatever pain the devil puts on me, because I want my faith to work for me.

That is my choice, but I don't impose that on my wife or my kids. I have no right to do that. They have free wills. I should teach them, and show them God's best, and Praise God, I have done that, but the choice is still theirs. After all, salvation is not based on going, or not going to the doctor, or having or not having insurance; but on the shed blood of Christ and our faith in that shed blood.

Once, Stephanie had an attack on her body in her ear, and the thing had her climbing the wall. We did all the things we knew how to do. We laid hands on her from stem to stern, we prayed, and we believed God, and she did herself. She is a faith child. She was using her faith all that she could, and doing everything that she could to keep from whimpering and crying, but you could see that thing was driving her buggy. So, about 2:00 o'clock in the morning, we had done all we could for her, and I got up, just as big as you please, and drove her to Children's Hospital. I was not looking to Children's Hospital as our healing source, but I figured that there was something that they could give her to deal with the symptoms until our faith took over and drove the thing out of her body. Why let a little nine year old lie there and suffer with her ears crawling, and she doesn't even know why she is hurting, when I've got the power and ability to do something about the pain that she is going through? I took her to the doctor, and they put some drops in her ears. Even the doctor didn't really know what was wrong. They figured it was some kind of infection. But I wasn't looking to the doctor for the healing. I was looking to the doctor to give her something whereby she could go to sleep. I couldn't make her sleep, and we were praying and believing God all we knew, but the manifestation was not there, and she was suffering.

I don't mind suffering. I'll suffer and take all the pain I can take for me, but I don't put that off on my wife and kids. If they want to do it, that is on them, and I let them make their decisions. If they say that they want to go to a doctor, I'll take them to the doctor. I am the father, and I am going to do everything I can to protect the investment God has given me. I don't see medicine, medication, doctors, hospitals, and nurses as anti-healing, or anti-God. I see them as merely assistants in the natural. Any doctor, nurse, or hospital will tell you they do all they know to relieve the pain and suffering. They are doing the best they know how to do. If they could do more, they would do it. They are working on it night and day.

That is not against divine healing. Admittedly, it is not the highest level of health. God is the highest level of health, but doctors are trying to help you. I believe that each person ought to be persuaded in his own mind, whether or not he wants to take medication. And I don't think that a father has the right to make that manda— tory on his family, and tell them, "You have to do it this way." If they come into agreement with you, and the two of you agree to do it, fine. But you shouldn't make a hard fast rule like that. It isn't fair.

Some guy will say, "It will hinder my faith."

That little baby is lying there, burning up with fever, and you are talking about whether or not it is going to hinder your faith. Don't be silly. You aren't even thinking about the baby. You are thinking about how it is going to look for you. Going to hinder your faith! How is that going to hinder your faith? Is your faith in the medicine?

"No."

Well, then, it can't hinder your faith. I will tell you what it will hinder. The only thing that giving some medication to that baby that is burning up with fever, is going to hinder, is the devil and demons from hurting that child. That is what it is going to hinder. It will hinder him from getting his kicks.

When I took Stephanie to the doctor, he put some drops in her ear, gave me a prescription to have filled, and told me to keep her home for the next couple of days. Now, at least she could go to sleep. She did not have that pain driving through her ear. You know what happened in the morning? We never did give her any medication. We never did get the prescription filled, and we didn't keep her home. She was well the next day. I don't see a thing in the world wrong with that.

Like I say, you do it your way. Just remember, when you start living in a world where there is no one else but you; when you drive your car where there are no other cars on the road but yours: when you are living within that little enclosed valley on your island, with no other cars on the road, no dogs, cats, chickens, or birds to cross your path: when you get into a place where there is nobody but you, and nobody else can be attacked by sickness — then you make that stand and say, "I'm not going to take any medication. I'm not going to the doctor, and I'm not going to have any insurance."

That is fine for you to do that, but I think if you are the head of the house, and if you have little children under you, you have a responsibility before God to take care of them to the extent that you can, and do anything that will not violate God's Word. I can't find any place in the Bible where it says, "Don't take medicine." I don't see where it says, "Don't have an operation." I do believe that there is a better way than that, but you have to get to that place. You have to grow to that point where you can do that. You don't start out believing after the doctor tells you that you have cancer. You had better go to the doctor, because I'll tell you right now, you are not going to operate in faith, you will be operating in desperation. If you were operating in faith, and knew anything about faith, you would not have accepted the cancer in the first place. The fact that you have that thing lets you know that you had better find a good surgeon, or somebody to stem the tide of that disease until your faith can be developed strong enough to drive it out of your body.

Now, I know that there have been some people who have been healed, but you watch and see, in 99% of the cases where people have been healed of cancer, it has been when the gifts of healings were operating. It was not that individual's own faith standing on the Word of God.

Check it out. You will find that is true. I believe in God's divine healing in terms of the gift of the Spirit operating, but according to 1 Corinthians 12:11, it says, "But all these worketh that one and the self-same Spirit, dividing to every man severally as he will." Gifts of healings work, but you don't know when it is going to work for you.

In the meantime, you are going to let that precious wife of yours die? Are you going to let the little child die? Just because you want to look super-spiritual to everybody around you, you are going to let your little child burn up with fever all night long, when you can do something about it? Shame on you.

We are talking about the practical aspects of faith. Is this *Faith, Foolishness, or Presumption?* Now, like I said, I am not going to go out and buy $5,000,000 worth of hospitalization. I don't need that. But I am going to have enough available so that if my wife says, "Look, I just don't feel like standing against any more pain. Man, I am hurting. I want you to take me to the doctor, and get me a shot." I can take her to that doctor.

Do you think I am going to tell her, "Well Honey, you are sinning if you get a shot. You are going to hell?" No! I'll tell her, "All right, if that is what you want to do. You know what the Word says." But I have no right to impose this on my wife, my children, or family. I have no right to force that on them to make them do what I do. I can make the decision for myself, and I have made my decision, but I should not make that mandatory for them and say to them, "You're not in faith. Go cancel your insurance."

What is the insurance for anyway? Simply to give the devil no place. I have seen people lose their homes, lose their life savings, and lose everything they had over a sickness, or a cancer, or a prolonged illness. Was it worth it?

Thank God, when your faith is mature and strong, you can do without the doctors and the insurance. That is why I tell you to use your faith now, on the little issues of life. Don't wait until you get cancer. Don't wait until the doctor tells you that it's incurable, but use your faith right now. Then when your faith is strong, the devil won't be able to make the cancer stick on you anyhow. But until that time, I don't think there is anything wrong in using doctors, medicine, or insurance if you need it. Praise God, it is available to you.

Faith should not be based on *not taking medicine*, or *not going to the doctor*, or *not having insurance*. It should be based on **God's Word**.

6

Family Obligations

In the last chapter we were talking about insurance. We will discuss it a little more as we look at *Family Obligations*. Many people have a problem with insurance. They say, "If you are going to live by faith you shouldn't have insurance." Where does it say that in the Bible? "But Brother Price, that is inconsistent. If I am trusting God, and believing God, then I don't need insurance." Right! If you were living on an island by yourself with nobody else to interact with, then it might be possible for you to live without any insurance. You wouldn't need any then, because it would be just you and God. But remember: you are not perfect, and neither do you live in a perfect environment. You live in an imperfect environment, and you are imperfect.

When it comes to other people, for instance, a husband having a wife and children. He is not only the head of the house, but he is responsible to take care of those people. Providing a home for them, and providing some security and protection for them: whatever is involved in taking care of them. He is obligated to do that because he is the head of the house.

Suppose your wife decides not to use her faith and the doctor tells her she has to have an operation or she is going to die. Suppose she is pregnant and has to have a Cesearean section and she doesn't choose to use her faith. What are you going to tell her? "You believe God or die, Honey?" Is that what you are going to say? Remember, if she is at the place where she knows how to use her own faith, and she chooses not to use it, you cannot make your faith work for her in that situation, because she is responsible to use her own faith. Suppose the doctor tells you it is going to cost you $5,000, and you have only $5 in your checking account. What are you going to do, let your wife die? These are the things that you have to consider.

You know as well as I that insurance is not going to stop anything from happening. That is foolish. Insurance is not going to stop you from having an automobile accident, and insurance is not going to keep you from dying. But there is one thing that it can do: it can keep from giving the enemy a place, Ephesians 4:27 says, "Neither give place to the devil." Why shouldn't you give the devil place? If you don't give the devil place, that means that you don't give the devil an opportunity. A good Scripture that shows why you shouldn't give the devil place is found in John 10:10; Jesus is speaking and He is contrasting the Good Shepherd with someone else. Jesus styles Himself as the Good Shepherd, but He says that there is another fellow that is loose in the world, and he is referred to as the devil. Jesus said, "The thief cometh, not but for to steal, and to kill, and to destroy: I am come that they might have life, and that they might have it more abundantly." The thief (the devil) comes for nothing but to steal, and to kill, and to destroy. That means that you have to be on guard against the thief. Now, insurance is not going to stop the thief, but it can give you a measure of protection against him, for your family and yourself.

"Why?"

Because satan works through people. He works through men. He is not going to come flying out of the sky, but he will work through people. And you know as well as I that in this society all you have to do is dent somebody's door and they are ready to claim "whiplash," and they are ready to sue you.

They never ask for just the amount to cover the doctor's bill. They want to get rich quick, Baby. They are going to sue you for everything that you have. You can count on your fingers the times anybody takes somebody to court, and all they want to do is get the car fixed, or just get their medical bills paid, and the doctor's bill, or just get compensation for the time that they missed work. No. It is always for $50,000. Even though you only did $5 worth of damage, they will sue for $50,000, because this is a very mercenary society that we live in. It seems as though everybody is trying to get something for nothing. Insurance can keep the devil from stealing everything that you have worked for all of your life to get. Some don't have much, anyway, but the devil would like to steal all that they have. Insurance doesn't stop him from coming against you, but it sure can give him a hard way to go when it comes to him stealing everything from you.

I have seen people who have lost their homes. They have worked for years, and the wife got sick, and the husband's insurance ran out. Even the medical insurance ran out. He had to end up liquidating everything that they had. He had to sell the house, and the car. Many people have lost everything they had from a sickness, because they didn't have enough insurance.

Now, you are saying, "But we don't believe in being sick." That is right! I don't either, but let me ask you this question. Since you have been operating in faith, have you ever been attacked with sickness and disease? Hasn't the devil tried to put some sickness on you? Suppose he puts a sickness or disease on your little child, and your little child cannot come against it, what then? Or suppose your wife decides not to use her faith, and you have no insurance, what then?

PEOPLE ARE AT VARIOUS STAGES OF SPIRITUAL GROWTH

I don't look to insurance, because insurance can't stop anything from happening. It can't stop the attacks from coming, but it can help to ward off the attacks. Keep in mind, people are at various stages of spiritual growth and development. Nobody starts out with the same degree of faith force in manifestation that they will have after they walk with the Lord for a period of time. Insurance can be a deterrent to the enemy, until the person's faith is sufficiently developed to the point of not needing any.

We live in an imperfect society. We had a situation happen right on the parking lot of the church, one day. A Christian man came to Bible class to study the Bible. He came to get more information about God. He came for a legitimate reason and purpose. He was there on the church grounds to study the Word of God, and because he was an imperfect human individual, he was trying to turn his car around, and he miscalculated and ran into somebody else's car — another Christian's car right there on the church grounds. Both Christian's were filled with the Spirit, yet one Christian hit the other Christian's car. He didn't mean to do it, but it was about $100 worth of damage. As I said, he didn't mean to do it, but you see we are imperfect. When it has to do with other people, your children or your wife, I believe that the head of the house has the responsibility of providing protection if he can. Somebody got angry at me once and said, "You know that's just not consistent. Walking by faith and having insurance: I just can't see that."

All right, let me ask you a question. Do you have a lock on the front door of your house? Do you have locks on your car? Do you have locks on your garage? Well, you know as well as I that a lock certainly doesn't stop a thief from coming in if he wants in, but I tell you what, if he is walking down the street, looking for a house to break into, and he gets to your house and finds it all locked up, as tight as a drum, and he goes next door and that house is wide open, he is going to go into the one that is the easiest to get into. If he really wanted to get into your house, the lock will not stop him, but the lock sure will discourage him, and it makes his job just a little bit harder. So, if it is all right to have a lock, it is all right to have insurance. The lock is insurance: you just don't pay any monthly premiums on it, but it is the same principle.

I am telling you, you had better lock that house up, because they will steal it. They will rip you off. The devil will rip you off. Why go through the hassle? My faith is not in the lock and that it is going to keep the criminals away, but that lock is going to make it hard for the thief to get in. I have my angels on guard, but suppose I'm not just right all the time. Suppose I do something dumb. Suppose I leave something open and don't realize it. We are not perfect. We use locks and insurance is the same thing. Not only that, but did you know that the Father God uses insurance? He has given us an insurance policy. In Ephesians 6:11, the Apostle Paul says, "Put on the whole armour of God (What for, Paul?), that ye may be able to stand against the wiles of the devil." He didn't say that you would be able to stop the devil from coming against you. Notice, he didn't say putting on the armour would *stop* him from coming, but it is going to stop him from getting through to you. That is an insurance policy as far as I am concerned. Look at vv. 14-16: "Stand therefore, having your loins girt about with truth and having on the breastplate of righteousness; And your feet shod with the preparation of the gospel of peace; Above all, taking the shield of faith (What do I need a shield of faith for?), wherewith ye shall be able to quench all the fiery darts of the wicked." Did you notice that the shield wasn't going to *stop* him from throwing them, but it is going to stop them from hurting you? If that isn't insurance, I don't know what it is. The only thing is, you don't have to pay the premium on it. Jesus has already paid it with His blood.

There are various reasons why it might be advisable for you to have insurance. I have it on my family, praise God! I don't trust it to stop anything from happening, but I am going to pin the devil down in that area.

I have a wife and kids, and I don't know when they might not want to believe God. And I've been there sometimes myself. I have been attacked to such a degree, and been in such pain, that I almost wished that I had never heard about faith and healing. Sometimes I would hurt so badly until I wanted to go to the doctor and let him give me a shot, and knock me out for six weeks, and that would have been easy. But I knew better. I knew that there would be no way that I could ever minister to the Body of Christ if it didn't work for me. If it doesn't work for me, I can't preach it. I just can't be phony.

Even though it is still true, it would be hard — I couldn't, with any real conviction, share with you what doesn't work for me. I couldn't tell you about believing Jesus for healing if I were sick myself. So, I had to stand. I made it up in my mind that I was going to stand; that I was going to hurt, and I knew that hurting couldn't kill me. But the devil wanted to scare me into thinking that the pain would kill me. Well, I just let the pain come. My wife can tell you; I crawled around on my bedroom floor, shouting and hollering at the top of my voice. I was in such pain I couldn't stand on my feet because my back was in such bad shape. I crawled on the floor. I had to crawl out of the bed. I had to crawl into the shower, and crawl up the wall and hold myself up to take a shower. I was under attack to that extent. But I refused to give in to it.

Everybody is not going to do that. Everybody is not going to make that kind of committment, and you can't force them to do so. They will take the path of least resistance.

I wanted my faith to work for me. I didn't want to have to call you up and have you pray for me. You might not feel like praying for me. You might not like the way I wear my hair, and you might decide not to pray for me. Or you may be on vacation somewhere and I couldn't get you on the telephone, or the telephone might be out of order. I would be up the creek in a boat with no oars. So, I learned how to believe God for myself.

But I have a wife and kids, and I am the head of the house. I have a responsibility to them. They may decide that they don't want to hassle that pain. After all, medication and doctors are not opposed to divine healing. They are trying to help you get well. The only thing is, they are only able to deal with the symptoms. Thank God, the Word of God deals with the cause of the thing. Praise the Lord, that is the difference. But dealing with the symptoms can sure put you in good stead to handle the cause.

Don't put yourself in bondage, or let anyone else put you in bondage.

There are many people who are putting their wives and children in bondage. They say, "You are hindering my faith. You can't go to the doctor." And they let that little baby lie there and burn up with fever. If you decide to do that for yourself, that is great. But it is neither right, nor Scriptural to impose that on your wife and children. Now, if they agree to it, fine. Then the two of you can agree together according to Matthew 18:19, and God will honor that. But suppose they don't: you need to at least make whatever you can available to them, because they are counting on you as their source in this life. Sure, they believe in God too, but you are the head of the house, so you need to think about it.

I don't say, go out and buy $5,000,000 worth of insurance. You don't need that, but get enough whereby the devil can't steal everything from you. Don't think that just because you don't have insurance, that you are operating in faith. And just because you have insurance doesn't mean that you are not operating in faith. Your faith is not based on whether you have or don't have. Your faith is based on whether or not you are operating on the Word of God.

When you get to a point where your faith and the faith of your wife and kids is operating to such an extent that it is impossible for the enemy to put any symptoms or pain on you, then perhaps you won't need any health, medical, or life insurance. Then you can do away with it if you wish. But I believe if it is available to you, and you can get it, there is nothing wrong with it.

I won't argue with you if you want to get rid of your insurance, and take all the locks off your house. I believe that God will honor that, but I also believe that He will honor the other. Especially when you have other people to consider and it isn't just you.

SHOULD I HAVE ANY LIFE INSURANCE?

Well, one thing for sure, if Jesus tarries you are going to die. And I'll tell you for sure, there are no funeral homes that I have ever heard of that will bury you for free. They want their money, and they want a lot of it. I have known people who thought that they were operating in faith, and they meant to do right, but they didn't stop to think about all the issues, and satan got in through somebody making a mistake, and they died. They didn't even have money for burial expenses. That doesn't glorify God. Then someone has to run around, scrounging, and begging, and hoping that somebody will help pay the bill. You should at least, have enough life insurance to bury yourself. I am not going to go out like some people, and put in for $100,000 worth of life insurance, but I am going to die, and there is no point in my wife even having to use her faith to believe to bury me. It costs money for the burying ground, and it costs money for the funeral, so a little insurance is no different than taking some money, putting it in the bank, and labeling it, "burial funds." Life insurance doesn't keep you alive, but praise God, it can be a blessing.

As I told you before, my wife and I had it tough during the early years of our marriage. Satan kept us bound, and we didn't even know that we didn't have to be bound. Nobody was telling us how to get out of bondage: all they were telling us was, "Say, 'Jesus, Jesus, Jesus!' Say, 'GLORY, GLORY, GLORY!' " Well, that won't pay any bills. And you know, when you are first married, all those insurance people find out about you, and here they come, wanting to sell you some insurance. What did I know about insurance? Nothing. I was young, and I wasn't thinking about dying. I figured, "Who needs insurance?"

Well, they scared me into taking out a little life insurance policy, and that life insurance policy was one of the things that helped us to survive. I borrowed on it.

If you have insurance, it is your money. You can borrow on it. It is like putting money in the bank. That's all. You are just giving the insurance companies the privilege to use it to do other things with it, but it is your money.

Again, I am saying, don't go out and buy all kinds of insurance. The point I am making is, don't let whether you have insurance, or do not have insurance, be the determinant as to whether you are operating in faith or not. You may be operating in *foolishness*, or you may be operating in *presumption*.

I had some life insurance before I came into the knowledge of faith and how to live by it, and I am not going to cancel it. It's not much, but my faith is not in that insurance to keep me alive. My faith is in the Word of God to keep me alive. But I know that I am going to die if Jesus doesn't come back. And if I should go the day before my wife goes, she is still going to have to make arrangements to bury me. Or if my wife and I go together, our kids are going to have to bury us. Well, why should they have to go out and get some money from somewhere. I just pay for my thing ahead of time, contrary to what some folks are saying: if Jesus tarries, I am going to die. And you are going to die. It has been 6,000 years from Adam and nobody has been able to overcome it yet, and you are not going to start now. You are going to die, so you might as well make preparations for it, and get it out of the way. That is all my insurance will do, pay for the burial. I don't think that that is a lack of faith.

I believe God, but these are things that have to do with everyday life that we live.

Somebody says, "Well, the Apostle Paul never had any insurance." Be fair, you know they didn't have insurance when Paul lived. There wasn't any Metropolitan Life Insurance Co. then. And that makes a difference.

I am not telling you to go out and get some insurance. I am trying to strike a balance, and get you out of bondage. I want to get you to a point where you realize that your faith ought to be based on the Word of God, while other things are incidental. Don't put yourself in bondage, and don't put your family in bondage, by making them feel like they are sinning if they have insurance. Whether you have it or not is irrelevant and immaterial. If you believe God, and your faith is strong enough you won't have to have any insurance, but just be sure you have enough faith to believe for you, your family, your wife, your kids, and all the other people that you are living around all the time. You will have to use your faith on all of them, to keep them from running into you. Sure, your angels will keep you from getting killed, I believe that. But Brother, I have used my faith and my cars have still been banged up. My family still banged up my cars.

The point I am making is this: Is it faith, necessarily, because I don't have insurance? Does it mean that I lack faith because I have insurance? I believe that it is irrelevant and immaterial. The question is really, "Where are you putting your trust?"

My trust is not in any insurance policies. They are just simply some available security measures that close the door to the enemy, and keeps him from coming through that method and wiping me out financially.

You make the decision. But I don't think that it is faith for a husband to just impose that on his wife and child, and especially newlyweds, by telling them that he is just going to believe God, and his faith is not even developed yet. It is just so easy to get those things, and when you get to a point where you don't need them, bless God — just go ahead and do without them. Don't make that a rule, and put others in bondage by making them feel that they are sinning if they do have insurance. You know as well as I, that locks are not going to keep burglars from breaking in if they really want to break in that house. And insurance is not going to keep you from having a wreck anymore than the shield of faith is going to keep the devil from throwing the darts at you. But it will help you to quench them when they get there. Praise the Lord!

7

What About Taking Medication?

A lot of people put undue strain upon their wives and children concerning healing and not taking medication. People may have a sick baby, and they could get it a shot and help the child. And they just sit there and let that baby suffer all night long, burning up with a fever, and the poor baby doesn't even know what is going on. What does that really prove? Does that prove you have faith, because you let your baby burn up with a fever? Is that an automatic sign that you have faith?

Well, I believe in healing, but I also have enough sense to know that all divine healing is not instantly manifested. So — what about the symptoms in between the time you pray and believe God, and until the physical manifestation comes?

You need to understand that all healing is not instantly manifested. I have seen people who were prayed for, and they thought that their act of faith was to throw away their glasses. They have thrown their eyeglasses away or jumped on them and broken them up, saying, "This is my act of faith, Bless God! I'm operating in faith, praise the Lord!" And they couldn't even see their hand in front of their face. They say, "Praise the Lord! I'm believing God for my healing. Oops! Excuse me, I didn't see you." I don't know why people get off in this. I have never taught it. Anybody that has been under this ministry has never heard me tell anybody to throw away their glasses. People get that on their own. They still don't understand the *faith message*. They still are relating faith to things, instead of relating faith to the Word.

A young lady came up to my wife and me one time, almost whimpering, almost in tears. She hardly had any friends now. Nobody would ride with her in her car. We couldn't figure out what in the world could be wrong. Finally, she said, "I claimed my healing for my eyes, but I can't see my hand in front of my face. But I don't know why nobody will ride with me in the car." I do! I know! Poor thing. That isn't *faith*, that is *foolishness*.

You may laugh at that, but I run into this all the time. Stop and think about this: In a case like this, your faith is not really in the Word of God: it is in not wearing glasses. Keep in mind that in divine healing, all divine healing is not instantly manifested. Especially faith healing. If you are making a claim by faith on God's Word for your healing, it doesn't always come instantly. If you go without your glasses in the meantime, what are you going to do? Kill somebody, run some pedestrian down, kill yourself and your own family, because you can't see your hand in front of your face? To go out there and drive, when you can't see is *foolishness*; not *faith*. What does wearing glasses or not wearing glasses have to do with your eyes being healed anyway? Nothing really — unless you put your faith in the glasses. If you put your faith in the glasses, and you take them off, then you are in trouble, because you have discarded your faith. But if your faith is in the Word of God, then let the Word of God be the evidence of things not seen, according to Hebrews 11:1. If you can do without your glasses in certain situations, don't wear them, but if you need to wear your glasses, then go ahead and wear them. And every time you put them on, say, "Praise God, I believe I am healed."

You may say, "Well, I just don't understand that." Right. That is because you still do not understand how faith works. You are basing your faith on *not* taking medication. You are basing your faith on *not* going to the doctor. You are basing your faith on *not* wearing glasses. You are basing your faith on *not* being in the wheel—chair, instead of on the Word of God. When you stop and think about it, you will know that wearing glasses doesn't heal your eyes, because if wearing glasses could heal your eyes, you would not have to pray. You would just wear your glasses. If you have worn glasses for any length of time, you know that your eyes do not, normally, get better because you wear glasses. They get weaker, and over the years you have to increase the strength of the prescription to compensate for the deterioration of your eyes. Therefore wearing glasses is irrelevant and immaterial to whether you are healed or not.

Many people still do not understand that if they put their faith in their glasses and they take them off, they are in serious trouble. They try to function as though they are healed, when in fact they are not healed yet. Because if you were healed, as a physical fact, you wouldn't have to wear glasses. If you actually had the healing physically manifested you would know it. For instance, as you read this book, and if you are wearing glasses, and if you were to remove your glasses, you would not be able to see. Then suddenly, the healing of your eyes manifested itself, do you know what would happen? You wouldn't be able to see through your glasses. Don't you think that you would know that your eyes were healed? Nobody would have to tell you to throw your glasses away!

"FAITH IS THE EVIDENCE . . . ."

The point that I am making is this: If you take your glasses off and you cannot see, then that ought to tell you that you are not healed yet, **as a physical fact**. Yes, you are healed **as a faith fact**, but remember, according to Hebrews 11:1, "Faith is the evidence of things not seen." It's not the fact that you don't have the glasses on. It says, "Now faith is the substance of things hoped for, the evidence of things not seen." It doesn't say that taking off your glasses is the evidence; it says that "faith is the evidence."

The very fact that you cannot see without your glasses ought to tell you that you are not healed yet as a physical fact. You wouldn't need the glasses if your healing were manifested. It is the same thing with the wheel chair.

Some people have hurt divine healing. They are just so anxious to see a miracle. I have seen them, and it has done a dis-service to the ministry of divine healing. Because of their actions they have put in the minds of many people that healing is just a "bunch of junk and a fake."

They will say, "Get up and walk in Jesus' name." And I have watched people get up and fall right on the floor. Let me tell you — if a person in a wheelchair believes he is healed by faith, it may not be a physical fact yet. When it does become a physical fact, nobody will have to tell him to, "Rise and walk in Jesus' name." They will rise and walk, because they will be the first to know that they are healed.

Whether you wear glasses, or ride around in a wheel—chair, if you believe that you have received your healing according to the Word of God, then it is a faith fact. It is not a physical fact yet. Because if it were a physical fact your urine would not show sugar to indicate that you need insulin. If you are believing God to heal you of diabetes, do not base your faith on not taking insulin, or any other kind of medication.

There was a celebrated case one time in the news. A boy died, and it set divine healing back in the minds of many people. An evangelist came to town and said, "You are healed in Jesus' name." It is said that the parents took the insulin away from the little boy, and he began to go into insulin shock.

The little boy said, "I need my medicine. I need my medicine. Give me my medicine:" and they wouldn't give it to him.

They didn't understand at all, and they thought that by taking away the medicine, healing would come. That is not *faith*. That is *presumption*.

WHAT CAN I DO, THEN?

Your initial, primary act of faith is the confession of your mouth of what you believe in your heart, based on the Word of God. You are not always able to act physically. No one should tell somebody to get out of the wheelchair. I'm sure the person in the wheelchair wants to, and has tried to get out of the chair, but until the healing takes place, he can't get out of that wheelchair. And he doesn't have to get out of the wheelchair to prove that he is healed as a faith fact. It is by the confession of his mouth, according to what the Word of God says. And when the power comes and the healing actually takes place physically, then he will get up.

Don't get into a bag of trying to prove that you are healed by not taking medication. If you can do without it, then don't take it, because the medication is not going to heal you anyhow: it helps the symptoms.

I don't choose to take any medication for myself. I have made it up in my mind, but that is just for me.

Don't try to do what somebody else does, unless you know the depth of their committment from their heart. You can't know that just by listening to them talk. It is nice to want to emulate somebody. It is nice to want to have a goal to shoot at, but you had better be sure that you can handle the action before you put yourself in that situation. I don't have anything against medicine, because medicine is not against divine healing. Medicine can work with divine healing. Medicine is not God's highest or best. There is a better way when you know how to use your faith. When you have developed your faith to such an extent that you can stand on the promises of God, then you won't need medicine.

That's the reason that I don't take medicine. If I needed some medicine, and I wanted to take it, I would take it. I wouldn't feel a thing about it, and it would not put me into bondage.

I am trying to help some of you husbands who put your wives and children into bondage, and make them suffer, just because you want to stand in faith. That is great for you to stand in faith, and I believe that you should do so, but I don't think that you should impose that on your wife or children. If they decide that they want to agree with you for their healing, do it. Wonderful. But I do not believe that you are right if you make them do so. That is not what the Bible tells you to do. They may not be ready for that.

The very fact that that little boy's body needed insulin shows you that he wasn't healed as a physical fact yet, because if he were healed he wouldn't have died.

THERE IS A DIFFERENCE BETWEEN A FAITH FACT AND A PHYSICAL FACT

When you believe God according to the Word of God, you have your healing as a faith fact, and the Word of God becomes the evidence of it. When you have it as a physical fact, then you don't need any evidence: you have it. Thank God, that medication is available if you need it. There is no point in you tossing to and fro all night long, in pain, and not sleeping, when you have a pain pill sitting right by your bed. God doesn't get any particular glory out of you whining and crying all night long, and you don't get any sleep. God doesn't get any glory out of that. However, if you, as an individual choose to do this on your own, that is different. I have made it up in my mind that I am going to act on God's Word. But that is my choice, and I will not impose it on my wife or my kids. They know what I believe, and they know what I stand for. They hear me preach it, and if they want to stand in faith they can. But I am not responsible for them standing in faith, and they are not responsible for me standing in faith.

If they want to go to the doctor, I'll take them. If they need medicine, and it will do them some good, I will give it to them, and won't feel a thing. Those are my kids, and that is my wife, and I love them. I don't want satan messing with them, and they may not be able or willing to make the kind of commitment that I have made. Everybody is just not going to make the same commitment.

There are some decisions that you have to make for yourself. And you cannot impose those decisions on somebody else, and call it "faith" because their will is involved. You may be acting *foolishly*, or you may even be getting over into *presumption*. When it comes to somebody else, their will is involved, and they can agree to it, then you can agree in prayer together. But just to impose it on them by saying, "You have to stand in faith, and you can't take any medicine," is not necessarily *faith*.

I am saying this to you if you are a young husband. It is great that you want to stand in faith, but you have to take into consideration your wife and your kids. Don't base your faith on *not taking medication*. Get that out of your mind. Medicine is not opposed to divine healing. It is all for it. It is just on a lower level, but God can work through medicine. I have seen people healed through medicine: it wasn't actually the medicine that healed them, but the medicine and the limited amount of faith that they put in God, gave God an avenue by which He could work through that medicine to make the thing come to pass. I have seen God work through surgeons: I've seen Him work through doctors. The doctor said, "Man, you'll be laid up for six weeks at least." And the person got out in three weeks. The doctor had to admit that it was a miracle. But it was a miracle on a lower level, because the person had to be cut on. He had to go to the doctor.

Remember, going to the doctor is not opposed to faith, nor is it opposed to divine healing: it is simply getting it on a lower level. It may cost you more, and you may end up with only one arm instead of two. But it doesn't mean that you have sinned. It is just on a lower level. But friend, if your faith is not operating at its highest level, one of the best friends you will ever have will be a good doctor.

LEARN TO USE YOUR FAITH ON SMALL THINGS

Learn how to use your faith on the next headache that comes to you. There may be some medical records on it, but I don't know of too many cases where people have died from headaches. There may be some cases, but on the average, a headache is usually not terminal.

Don't wait until the doctor takes a biopsy and tells you that it is malignant, to believe God for your healing of cancer. Because you will not be coming in faith: you will be coming in desperation. Start using your faith on the next pain that tries to approach your head. Determine, "I'll not take any Bufferin, or Anacin tablets for it. I am going to use my faith. I am going to build my faith." If you can't believe for a headache, there is no way in the world that you are going to believe God for the healing of a terminal cancer.

I STARTED USING MY FAITH ON SMALL THINGS

I started using my faith on colds: just the common cold. I started believing God. I stopped taking patent medicines for cold symptoms. I wouldn't accept the symptoms, or take any medication. I stood against it even though I had some miserable days, and times. But I was determined that I wanted to use my faith, and I knew that ordinarily a cold wasn't going to kill me. I can stand that, even though it was painful in many of the physical aspects of it. But I was determined that I wanted to learn to stand in faith. I used my faith on the colds, and I used it on the flu. I used my faith on the little issues of life that weren't terminal situations. Now, I have my faith moving. I developed my faith to the point that it drove a tumor out of my body. It made a tumor diasppear out of my body. And I say to you, learn how to use the principles of faith. Learn on the next headache that you get. Instead of taking the pills, use your faith. There is nothing wrong with taking the pills: don't get into bondage over that. But the point that I am making is, the only way that you will learn to use your faith is to use it. That is how your faith grows: when you use it. Use your faith on something that is not terminal, and then when the devil tries to approch you with cancer, or something else that is terminal, you can stand against him with no sweat. Why? Because you will have developed your faith to the point where it is working for you.

There are very few people that I've ever seen, who have been healed after the doctor told them that they had terminal cancer, by using *their faith*. If they were healed, it was usually the *gifts of healings* that operated through somebody's ministry like the late Kathryn Kuhlman type of ministry. That was not faith healing: that was the *gifts of healings*, and they operate as *the Spirit wills*, not as we will. And the thing about it is, you never know when the Spirit wills. But, thank God, you don't have to wait until the Spirit wills. God always wills through His Word. So learn how to use your faith on the little issues of life. But do not impose your faith on your family, your wife or your children, just because you want to believe God. Give them the benefit of making that decision. And if so, fine. But if they need medicine then give it to them. If my kids, or my wife wants some medication, I'll buy it for them and I just praise God that I am in a position where I can afford to buy it now, if I need it. I am not going to be so foolish as to think that satan doesn't try to put that stuff on me, because he does. And I never know when my wife may decide that she doesn't want to fight it anymore. She may say, "Give me a shot, and let me go to bed for a few days and forget it. I don't want to stand in faith." It is work to stand in faith. It is going to cost you something to stand against the enemy. He will bring the stuff on your body and put thoughts in your mind to make you think that you are going to die. He will try to run you scared. It is a constant battle. And sometimes people don't want to fight anymore.

If you have a family, you have a responsibility to them. It is not a sin to use medication. Like I said, it is not in opposition to divine healing. Medicine is trying to make you well, but it is just on a lower level. If you will learn how to use your faith on the little issues that are not terminal, you can grow to the point where you won't need any medicine.

I haven't taken any medicine in seven years, and I don't plan to do so. I can say that for myself, because I can decide what I do. But I can't say that for my wife. I trust that she will believe like I do. I trust that my kids will also.

I have seen this too often. Some children, even though they grow up around the faith message, and even though they see Dad operate in it, it is (a lot of times) just a little easier to let Dad do it: Operate on the parents' faith. It is easier to let somebody else do it. But oh, what a joy it is to learn how to do it for yourself. What a joy to learn how to stand on God's Word for yourself. So don't let medication be the thing that decides whether you are operating in faith or not, and don't let the lack of medication be the determining factor. Your faith is based on God's Word. You stand on the Word of God. If you need a crutch or something to help you along, then praise God, hobble along until you get your faith moving to the point where you don't need the crutch.

GET THAT FAITH DEVELOPED FIRST

Don't put yourself in bondage, and don't open the door for the enemy to kill you, when your faith is not sufficiently developed to handle the situations that come against you. Don't just sit there and say, "Well, I'm just going to tough it out." Maybe you can, but you had better know that you can. You had better know your own commitments. You had better know that you are not going to get scared, half-way through, and let the devil scare you off.

Like some symptoms, they won't look so good, and you need to be careful. Somebody will say, "I don't need that." Well, praise the Lord, it may not be for you. But it is for some, because I run into this problem over and over again. People are basing their faith on *not* taking medication. They are not basing their faith on the Word of God. Basing your faith on not taking medication is not a good enough place to put your faith.

Put your faith on the Word of God. Develop your faith. Use your faith, and then you won't need the medication. You won't need the insurance. You won't need the other things. But don't let the fact that you use those things or don't use them, be the determinant as to whether you are operating in faith, or not. It may not be faith. For you, it may be foolishness at that time, because if your faith is not sufficiently developed it's not going to work.

I have watched people die, and my heart went out to them, but their faith was not developed, and it couldn't bring the healing to pass, and they died. It wasn't the will of God that they die, but their faith wasn't sufficiently developed. Because they didn't know about it, or they didn't take the time to develop their faith on the little issues of life when they had the opportunity. They wanted to be like so and so. "I'm not going to do this. I'm not going to take any medication. I'm not going to have any insurance, and I'm not going to do this, that, or the other." And I have watched people get wiped out on that.

Start out little, and grow, and grow, and grow, and grow, and when you grow — praise God! it will be well worth it.

8

Family Relationships

Sometimes, Christians hear the Word of God, concerning faith, and they deal with the Holy Ghost, and they actually become so "super-scriptural," that they neglect the family relationships. They neglect the responsibilities of the home. So, we want to find out is this *Faith*, or is it *Foolishness*, or is it *Presumption?*

Paul says in Ephesians 5:31; "For this cause shall a man leave his father and mother, and shall be joined unto his wife, and they two shall be one flesh." And *they shall be one flesh.* In other words, in the sight of God they become *one.* Therefore, if they are *one,* they each must have the same care, one for the other. They should be seeing each other as *one* — as a unit. Too often Christians who get so "super-spiritual," think that they are operating *in faith*, and suddenly, they do not have time for the common things, like cleaning up the house, washing dishes, or mowing the lawn, taking out the trash, or fixing a broken screen, or something like that. They don't have time: they say, "I have to study the Word. I have to be in prayer. I have to get alone with the Lord." Is that *Faith, Foolishness, Or Presumption?*

I don't know why, but it seems to me that there are more women than men who believe that they are so *super-spiritual* that they are *too holy* for sex. They say, "That is mundane. That is just ordinary. I have to be more spiritual. I have to pray in the spirit . . . ." This is one of the things that really causes a disaster in the home. Because these Christian women come into the knowledge of God, and get Spirit-filled, and their husbands are not yet saved. And they treat their husbands like dogs.

Now Lady, he may be a dog, but you shouldn't treat him like a dog. It is unfortunate that some husbands are dogs: they do act like dogs. But you are going to have to learn that you can't win him by treating him like a dog. You are going to have to win him by treating him like he is somebody, because to God — he is somebody. He is worth enough that God permitted the blood of His only Son to be shed to redeem that man; so he must be worth something. He is worth saving if he was worth Jesus dying for him. If God sees something in him, then you had better start seeing something in him. And perhaps you will have a little more victory in winning him to Christ if you start treating him as though he were worth something, instead of looking down your nose at him, as though you were so *super-spiritual.*

In counseling with people, I run into this area where the wife doesn't want to be a wife in the area of sex any more. She is out on the street *casting out demons.* I am not as much aware of so many men in this same situation, but I do know of some of them too. They get so *super-spiritual* that they just go to work, come home, get their Bibles, go lock themselves up in the car, or garage, or somewhere, and they just stay out there all night, listening to tapes, and reading the Word and praying. And the poor wife has been waiting for him all day long, but he does not have time for her, because he is so *super-spiritual.* He doesn't have time for such common things as husband-wife relationships. He doesn't realize that he is opening the door for the enemy to come in and mess up his home.

God never intended for you to become so *super-spiritual* that you cannot take care of family relationships. When you neglect that, without realizing it, you are giving the enemy an advantage over you. You should not get that holy. You should not think that sex is unholy. When it is done in the proper context of the marriage relationship, it is the most beautiful physical relationship that you will ever experience. If it is not beautiful with you, then you are missing something.

This is where we live, and one of the greatest problems that I run into in counseling people is this business of sexual relationships between a husband and wife. Some of them have become so *super-spiritual* that they just don't have time for that. Some men are mistreating their wives, and the wives are mistreating their husbands, and they are not allowing proper time for that. There is plenty of time. There are 24 hours in a day! You can squeeze in a little time, and you are going to have to do it, if you want the relationship to work right, because that is a part of the marriage relationship.

LEARN TO REGIMENT YOUR TIME

Some people say, "Well, I have to get alone with the Lord, and I don't have time for that." I want to show you that the Bible does not tell you that. In fact, the Bible tells you just the opposite. What you have to do is learn to regiment your time; learn how to discipline yourself, as far as time is concerned. When you do, I'll guarantee you that you will find plenty of time to do all the things that need to be done, and do them in style. Somehow, we have gotten the idea that to be spiritual means that you have to divorce yourself from all the natural things in life. No. This is where we live. You say, "I can't write any checks and pay any bills. I have to get alone with the Lord. Mowing the lawn is unspiritual." No, it is all a part and parcel of the whole package of life, and you need to learn how to relate it to the Word of God.

We read in Ephesians 5:31 where ". . . they shall be one flesh." Let us look at another Scripture that goes right along with this husband and wife business of becoming so *super-spiritual* that they neglect their family obligations. In 1 Corinthians, chapter 7, we begin with verse 2, and read, "Nevertheless, to avoid fornication, let every man have his own wife, and let every woman have her own husband." Now, you know as well as I do, or if you don't know, you need to find out, that fornication has to do with sexual intercourse, usually between people that are not married. That shows you right there that God is not opposed to sexual intercourse, because if He were opposed to sexual intercourse, He would have made no contingencies for you to perform it. He is telling you that when you do it outside of the context of marriage, you are in sin. But He is going to show you how you can be a part of that, and have it in its proper context; in marriage. Notice, He said, "Nevertheless, to avoid fornication, let every man have his own wife, and let every woman have her own husband." Husbands; wives, that is godly. That is the will of God, that there be husbands and wives. He goes on to say, "Let the husband render unto the wife due benevolence; and likewise also the wife unto the husband. The wife hath not power of her own body, but the husband: and likewise also the husband hath not power of his own body, but the wife."

There is a teaching that is prevalent in this Charismatic renewal about the business of submission. Some men want to use this against their wives and they say, "Well, you are supposed to submit." What they fail to realize is that in many instances they have taken the word *submit* and have given it the same meaning as the word *domination*. *Submission* does not mean *domination*. The word *submit*, literally, in the Greek, means "yield unto the other." It means to "yield to the other person."

And the Bible does not just say for wives to submit to the husbands, but it says that both the husband and the wife should submit one to the other on an equality. *Submission* simply means "yielding to the other person." In other words, you seek to make the other person happy instead of yourself.

Some men have the idea that submission means that they can give orders to their wives, and they tell them what to do, and run them around like robots. That is not according to the Bible. That is not *submission*: that is *domination*. God does not intend for any man to dominate another man. You are not to be dominated by your husband, or dominated by your wife. "Let the husband render unto the wife due benevolence: and likewise also the wife unto the husband" (v. 3). He tells us in v. 4; "The wife hath not power of her own body, but the husband: and likewise also the husband hath not power of his own body, but the wife." What is he saying? He is saying that it should be a mutually agreed situation. It should either be mutually agreed to do or not to do, but it should not be one person telling the other person that this is the way it has to be. There ought to be an agreement between the two. And unless there is an agreement between them, it is not really going to work out right. I have sat across the desk from many people over the years, and that is one of the areas where they are really messed up — but good. One thinks that he is supposed to tell the other what to do, when it should be a mutually agreed situation.

Verse 5 says, "Defraud ye not one the other, except it be with consent for a time, that ye may give yourselves to fasting and prayer; and come together again, that satan tempt you not for you incontinency." *Incontinency*, in the Greek, literally means "lack of control, or lack of control over yourself." All right, he said, "Defraud ye not one the other, except it be with consent . . . ." If the husband is

going to deny his wife her husbandly affection and attention, and the wife likewise, it should only be done when
the two of them agree to it. One does not have any right
to just go off somewhere alone, lock himself, or herself, up
with the Word, and deny the wife, or husband. It should
be a mutually agreed situation, where they agree, "We
will do it for this period of time." Then he says, ". . . come
back together so you won't be tempted by the enemy,"
because temptation is going to come in that area if you are
not careful. He is giving you a way that you can *ward off*
that problem. When you get to the point where you are so
super-spiritual that you don't have time for family
relationships, be careful.

YOUR CHILDREN REQUIRE ATTENTION

Another problem area is where parents get so
spiritual that they don't have time for their children. I
have seen many young people, and a lot of children who
are very *uptight* in certain situations. Because the mother
and father are so busy doing the other things that they
never have any time for the children. Children are a part
of the family relationship, and it is not unholy or
unspiritual. No: it is very spiritual. You can bring your
children, your family into that same relationship, and
there can be a sharing together. And there had better be
a sharing together, or you are going to have trouble in
your home.

That is really not *faith* when you say, "I am just going
to pray and read the Bible — 15 chapters a day, and I'm
going to spend 5 hours in prayer every day." Well, that is
great, if you are single. But you can't always do that when
you've got a wife and kids. You have to give them some
attention and some time. If you don't, satan will get in
through that area and cause confusion within the home. It
is not unspiritual and unscriptural to be in love with your

wife, or in love with your husband, or in love with your children and have some time of fellowship with them.

He said in the above Scripture verse, "Defraud ye not one the other, except it be with consent." That means that the two of you ought to agree on it, and you ought to work out your schedule to where that is included in it, just like bathing, brushing your teeth, or going to work is included. That ought to be a very precious part of the relationship. And that is not *Faith;* that is *Foolishness* when you neglect these things.

A WORD TO THE WISE . . . .

The wise man takes care of the home, and that means the wise woman too. I would to God that some women would stop running around to every prayer service: going to meetings here, and meetings there, and all the time they are leaving their husbands and children at home.

The husband has to come home from work and cook his own dinner because the wife is out "casting out demons." I believe in casting out demons, but I also believe in taking care of the home. Get your home straightened out and you will be able to cast out demons. Amen!

You need to watch it there. Is that *Faith, Foolishness, Or Presumption?* It is *Foolishness* in many cases, and it also borders on *Presumption,* because Paul said, the only reason we ought to defraud each other (deny each other) would be when we do it by consent, to give ourselves to prayer and fasting. So — if you are not fasting and praying, get it together. It is not necessarily Faith because you are reading the Bible. You could be operating in *Foolishness* or *Presumption.* You ought to get it together and you will find that you will have a very

sweet relationship at home, and even spiritual things will
operate a lot better.

SHOULD HUSBANDS AND WIVES ALWAYS
STUDY THE WORD TOGETHER

The idea that husbands and wives have to pray and
read the Bible together is another area that causes
problems. It is not necessary to pray together!

"Oh?"

No. The old adage, "The family that prays together
stays together," is not necessarily true. There is more to
it than just praying together to keep the family together.
You may have different ways of doing it.

Now, with my wife and I, there are times when we
pray together when we are agreeing on something. But in
terms of our daily prayer time, we rarely pray together.
Our praying habits are different. She does not pray like I
pray. I pray at a certain time, and she prays at a certain
time. We do not read the Bible together, and I believe
that we have a beautiful relationship. There is nothing
wrong with our relationship just because we don't pray
and read the Bible together. Now, it is fine if you want to
do it together, and if you can work it out. But you should
not break up or jeopardize the relationship just because
you don't. Thinking that you are acting in *Faith* just
because you pray together does not necessarily mean that
it is in *Faith*. You have to learn what works best for you
and then do that. It is not an automatic rule that you have
to always pray together, or try to have a family altar (kids
and everybody). Sometimes the wife has things to do, or
the husband has things to do, and the children have things
to do. It is just not always convenient or appropriate.
Years ago, they could do it. They had no where to go: the
wife was not working, and there wasn't much else to do,

but pray together. The kids didn't have too much to do except stay home, and the man was the only one who was working.

Today, there are many things in our society that are different. If you can manage this, wonderful! But don't think that just because you do, that that means it is a *Faith* situation, just because you do pray together. You could go through some prescribed pattern just as a ritual and still gain nothing from it. Learn what works best for you.

My wife has to have her cup of coffee in the mornings. In fact, it takes her a little while to wake up. What I mean by that is, she will be up and moving, but she is not really awake yet. It takes a little time before all of her faculties are functioning properly. She likes to go into the kitchen and turn on the coffee pot, sit down, have a cup of coffee, and then she is ready to go. She is ready to read the Bible; she's ready to pray. But as soon as my eyes pop open and my feet hit the floor, I am awake, instantaneously. I am ready to pray, and I am going to pray then. Because if I don't pray then, I won't pray. Do you know why? People will see to it that I don't pray. They will be calling me on the telephone all day, and all night. I won't get to pray if I don't do it first. That's right. And sometimes, if I have to, I take the telephone off the hook. I am not going to be disturbed while I am praying. I pray early in the morning. That's the first thing that I do. Of course, I have to have my orange juice first. But I don't need that to wake up. That is just the way I start putting a little something in my stomach. I get a glass of orange juice and I come back and get in the bed, under the covers, where it is warm and pray. That's right.

"Oh, Brother Price, you have to be on your knees to pray."

Who says so? Find me a chapter and verse where it says that you have to be on your knees to pray. You don't even have to have your eyes closed to pray. Read the 11th chapter of the Gospel of John. The Bible says, "Jesus lifted up His eyes to heaven and said, Father, I thank thee that thou hast heard me. And thou hearest me always, and for the benefit of those who stand around, I said it. Lazarus, come out of there!" (Author's translation). Praise God! and He raised Lazarus from the dead. The only reason that you have your eyes closed is to keep yourself from being distracted by what is going on around you. Your eyes being open or closed has nothing to do with it. What is the blind man going to do? He can't see. It is not the posture of prayer: whether you are on your knees, lying on your back, standing on your head, or doing a hand stand against the wall; it doesn't make any difference. I have done that. I have gotten up at 5:00 a.m., getting down on my hands and knees, and freezing my tail off, and all the time, I was thinking about when I could get up and get warm. I didn't have my mind on praying, so I now pray in bed. There is no point in freezing, and I lie under the covers and pray. God hears me.

God does not hear you because you are on your knees. He hears you because you are coming in faith. He hears you because you come according to His Word.

God hears me just as quickly when I have on my pajamas as He does when I am wearing a suit. He hears me just as quickly when I am on my knees, standing up, or riding in the car, or running and jumping — whatever I am doing.

Find out what works best for you and operate in that. Don't think that it is an act of faith simply because you pray with your husband or wife. If it works out that way, wonderful. That is great to do it that way. But that is not a necessity to make it work, and it does not mean that it's not faith because you don't do that.

Don't put any undue stress or burden upon your wife or husband by thinking that because they don't pray with you, or read the Bible with you, that they are unspiritual. It doesn't make any difference. Find out what works best for the two of you.

My wife reads while drinking a cup of coffee. She likes to read at the table. My habits are different than hers. So we hardly ever read or pray together. I can't remember the last time we prayed together in a general way: except when we were praying to agree on something. It has been years since we have read the Bible together only because our reading habits are different. But she is not any less spiritual than I am. Just because we don't read the Bible together. If you will find out what works best for you, and then do that, you will gain the benefit from it.

SUPER—SPIRITUAL SLOPPY RAG DOLLS OPEN THE DOOR TO THE ENEMY

Lady, or Gentleman, if you are so *super—spiritual*, super—holy, that you are too holy for sexual relationships, or the physical aspect of your marriage relationship, you are opening the door for the enemy to get in. And I may as well say this while I am at it, I notice sometimes that women will get real spiritual, and then they start looking like sloppy rag dolls, and they are too holy to comb their hair now. They are too *super—spiritual* to go to bed with their hair in rollers.

"My God! That's not very spiritual, Brother Price."

And so, you are in such a hurry to go out and cast out demons that you start wearing wigs all the time. Now, wigs are all right; I'm not knocking wigs, but I want you to know that your husband wants to see the real you. He wants to see you, and he knew what your hair was like when he married you, unless you had a wig on at the wedding. Fix yourself up. Be presentable to your husband. Husband, you be presentable to your wife. Look like who you really are, one of the "King's Kids." Take care of yourself. Comb your hair. Wash your face and brush your teeth. If you need a little Scope, use it. That's right! People think that because you get spiritual and you start walking in faith, you don't have time to comb your hair, you don't have time to bathe, you don't have to use deodorant, and you don't have time to dress up. That is not *Faith*, that is *Foolishness*.

If you say, "I wonder why my wife (husband) doesn't respond to me like she used to?" you are probably not treating her like you used to. She could not grab the door handle before you were out of your side, locked the door, ran around the car, and opened the door for her. Threw your coat down so she could walk on it, and she would not get her dainty little feet wet walking across the street. Now — you just get out of the car, close the door, don't even look back to see if she got out of the car. She may be locked in the car and can't get out, and you are gone! And you wonder why she doesn't respond. You used to come over to her house and before you would get to the door and knock on the door, you would reach into your pocket and pull out your Banaca Blast (spray). Now, you don't even brush your teeth, and you wonder why she doesn't want to kiss you. Ask me! I'll tell you why. It may sound funny, but it's not. These are areas where we live, and you should learn that you cannot disassociate your spirituality with common decency and common sense, in relationships one with the other. All of these things go to together.

Wife: When you were going with "Him!" you wanted to win him. I mean you watched your diet. You were going to be sure you were a certain size and you weren't going to get any bigger. You were going to look good for your man, and you bought the best dresses, and the stuff that made you look your best. Now that you have arrived at super-spirituality, you don't care how you look. Fat, sloppy, and overweight: eating those bon-bons, and chocolate candy. That's right! You were a petite size 9, and now you have gone to a size 18, and wonder how come he is not turned on anymore.

"Well, I'm spiritual, I pray in tongues."

Lose some weight!

Let's get back to the men. The same thing goes for some of those pot-bellied rascals. That's right! They (fat, out of shape rascals) wonder why she doesn't fall into a swoon when they come home. They come in with a big fat belly sticking out! And you may laugh at this, but I see this happening in people's lives. Somehow, they think that just because they get filled with the Spirit, they are supposed to be operating in faith, and these other things do not matter! Many times people are not able to express these things and they just put up with them, and they go on and on, and on. And satan uses that like a festering sore, and it brings on a bad situation way down the line, whereas if you will deal with it now, it will be a most beautiful relationship.

All of these things go together, Friend. Because you get over into the realm of faith doesn't mean that you leave the realm of reality. Spiritual and material reality go hand in hand. If you are a little too spiritual for your husband, or wife, you had better reappraise the situation, or you are going to find yourself at home without a husband, or wife, because satan has somebody out there

who will steal him, or her. Men, you have a good investment there. Good women are hard to find. And men are
even harder to find. Many times when you look over the
fence, and the grass looks greener over there, remember
you have spent 15 years with this rascal. You just now
have him trained, and you are going to start over with
another one? You are going to have the same problems
you had before. Protect the investment you have now.
You have invested a lot in that marriage. AMEN!

This is where you live. Is it *Faith, Foolishness, Or
Presumption?* When you get so spiritual that you don't
have time for family responsibilities, that's not *Faith.*
Sometimes it is abject *Foolishness*, and sometimes it even
borders on *Presumption.*

DEODORANT ? TO USE OR NOT TO USE?

Somebody says, "Well, I'm not going to bathe or use
deodorant. I'm going to believe that I'm not going to
smell." There are some people who really believe that.
You can tell! You see, that's what's wrong. Nobody wants
to talk about reality. They say, "Well, you shouldn't talk
about . . . ." Why not? That's where people live. If people
had been properly instructed you wouldn't find anybody
smelling. Nobody wants to be deliberately offensive.
Because nobody has taken the time in loving-kindness to
tell them about it, they have done their own thing. Well,
if you don't bathe, and if you don't use deodorant, you are
going to smell. If you want to smell nice, you are going to
have to use something nice. You are going to have to take
some precaution and take care of yourself.

Many of you Christians need to learn to take care of
yourselves. You get so super-spiritual and you say, "What
can I do to win my husband — to win my wife?" You can
be the sweetest, nicest, most beautiful thing that he ever
saw in his life, and you can be the trimmest, most loving

hunk of man she ever saw. That will help. At least it won't turn them off. Sometimes the reason they don't come more quickly is because you have not done too much to encourage them to come. You nag and whine after them, but you are not taking care of the things that you ought to take care of, and it can be a stumbling block.

It is not Faith, just because you say that something is not going to happen when you are doing everything in the world to produce that result. You are going to reap what you sow. And you know as well as I, that if you don't bathe, you are going to sweat and you are going to smell bad, if you don't use some deodorant.

That is not *Faith;* that is *Foolishness.*

9

Casting Out Calories!

As we continue our discussion of Is It *Faith, Foolishness, Or Presumption?* concerning family relationships, we will look at the situation of overeating. Somebody told me a story one time that fits right in with this situation. Some people were sitting around the table and one person prayed this prayer: "I bind all of the calories in the food, and cast them out in Jesus' name. And I believe that I can eat this food and not get fat."

The other person said, "This kind (fat) comes out only through prayer and fasting!" Of course you know that fasting is not eating!

A lot of people have the silly idea that they can overeat and not get fat. My wife and I were in a certain place one time, and we were having dinner with some people. We could look at one girl, and tell that she was overweight. When she prayed over the food, she cast out the calories!

Some people say, "Mark 11:24 says, 'What things soever ye desire when ye pray, believe that ye receive them, and ye shall have them.' I believe that I can eat as much of this cherry pie as I want and it is not going to make me fat."

That is not the meaning of Mark 11:24. That is not *Faith:* that is absolute *Foolishness!* If you eat fattening food, you are going to get fat, and you might as well get ready for it.

Let's find out what the Bible says about this situation. I hear these things with my own ears. "Casting out calories!" They have taken the Scriptures and have misappropriated and misapplied them, where Jesus said, "Whatever you bind on earth is bound in heaven. Whatever you loose on earth is loosed in heaven, and in my name you shall cast out demons." So they lay hands on the food when they get ready to eat, and they are going to "Cast out the calories, and eat all they want and not get fat." That is not *Faith:* that is *Foolishness*, and if you keep on eating, you are going to get fatter and fatter.

It says in Proverbs 23:2, "Put a knife to thy throat, if thou be a man given to appetite." Yeah, if you want to know what to do about that overeating, do what the Bible says. And when it says "man," it also speaks of women. God is saying to you, if you have an appetite and you can't control it, then you had better get a knife and put it to your throat. When you sit down and start gluttonizing yourself, you will think twice about that third piece of apple pie. It is Foolishness if you think you are going to eat, eat, eat, and not get fat. You are going to get fat.

"Well, I've always been able to eat a lot, and I never gain weight."

You keep on living. You may not get as big as some, but if you keep on living, you are going to get a pot-belly. You may be thin, but if you keep on stuffing yourself, you are going to get a belly.

I used to be that way. I could eat all I wanted. I used to eat 12 hot cakes at one time, three hamburgers and a malt, when I was going to high school. I played hard and fast; so I burned up the calories. I can't eat like that now. If I do, it turns to fat, Baby, F-A-T — fat.

Now here, the Bible says, "Put a knife to your throat if you be a man or a woman given to appetite." If your appetite has a hold on you, you had better get a hold on it, or it will ruin you.

Praying over your food, "In the name of Jesus, I cast these calories out. Come out in Jesus' name:" is not *Faith*. It is *Foolishness*. You need to bring your body under. It's not *Faith* to think you can pray and eat whatever you want.

These people who say, "I don't eat very much." Come on, you are really fooling yourself, and satan is going to keep that thing on you. You see a lot of styles of clothes that you would like to wear, and you can't wear them because you look like a blimp in them. You don't even like yourself. When you get out of shape, you don't look good in your clothes.

I like to go shopping with my wife, because nobody knows how she looks better than I do. I always go shopping with her. In fact most of the time I pick out her clothes. Those sales people will say, "Darling, it looks just fine. It's is just made for you, Darling: it's beautiful."

But I don't like it, and the sales people can't understand why I don't like it. I say, "I said, I don't like it. I'm paying, and I get what I like."

Sometimes while my wife is in the dressing room, I see some of these ladies come in the store, and my heart goes out to them. I can see them just drooling. They look at certain sizes and certain designs of dresses, and I know that they would like to wear them, but then they look at themselves in the mirror, and they have to go over to the fat girl's sizes, and there is not much to choose from. They really don't want to be fat, but they have never learned to put the knife to their throats. They have never learned to control their appetites. I am not talking about women of the world. I am talking about Christian women.

Read what it says in 1 Corinthians 9:27: "But I keep under my body, and bring it into subjection: lest that by any means, when I have preached to others, I myself should be a castaway." This is the great Apostle Paul talking. He says, "But I keep under my body, and bring it into subjection . . . ." meaning that if I don't put some controls on my flesh, it is going to get out of control. It is my responsibility to control myself, to control my body. No, that's not *Faith* when you pray over food and command the calories to leave. That's not *Faith*, that is *Foolishness*.

You need to learn how to take control of your body, and I'll guarantee you one thing, if you stop eating, you will start losing weight. Non-eating will produce non-weight. There is only one thing that produces weight, unless you have some kind of glandular problem, but that is easy to deal with. You can get healed. If you have glands that are running wild, you can pray over that and get healed: there is no problem there. But if you are over-weight, you just keep on gaining weight, and you say that you are not eating, you are really *conning* yourself.

An automobile runs on gasoline, that is the fuel. Have you ever noticed that little guage on your dash board that reads *full* and *empty*? Have you ever noticed how the gasoline goes from *full* to *empty*. It is not because there is a hole in your gas tank. It is because that monster runs on gasoline. It eats it as fuel. That is how it gets its power. It burns the fuel. That is the way your body uses your food that you eat. Food is fuel for your body. If you put into your body, just enough fuel for it to run on, then your body will burn it up and there won't be any increase in weight.

On the otherhand, if you cram more in than your body needs to run on, it will store the excess as fat. You can pray all you want to, but you will get fat if you don't put a knife to your throat. You will have to learn how to put your body under and keep it under, and control it, or else it will control you.

You say, "I'm just going to pray over the food, and in Jesus' name, I'm going to cast out those calories." That won't work. You can pray all you want. You can claim Mark 11:24 all you want, but if you keep on eating, you are going to keep on getting bigger and bigger. That is not *Faith*, that is *Foolishness*.

I'm not that big, but I have to control my diet. My wife and I control our calorie intake. We watch out diet. I'm not very large, but I can get a pot-belly very quickly. When I was younger, my stomach was like a washboard, hard as a rock. I'm getting it like that again. But for awhile it was getting ridiculous. I could not get my pants on comfortably. I would hold my breath and put on my pants. I had a particular pair of pants, and one day, I noticed that those pants were so tight, and I said, "What in the world is this?" I looked in the mirror sideways and I did not like what I saw: a fat, sloppy preacher. I don't like fat, sloppy preachers! And I'm not going to be one.

We started cutting down on our food intake, and going easy on things like rice and potatoes, which we really like.

You have to keep your body under, or it will get out of control. You can pray and have all the people in the world agreeing that you won't get fat, but that is not Faith. There is only one way you are going to stop getting fat, and that is by cutting down on your food intake. Curb your diet: curb your intake. Take control of that body and don't let it dominate you.

That is right: get yourself together. It will take discipline. And ladies, you just look better in a size 10 than you do in a size 18. I don't care what anybody says.

So it is not *Faith* just to say you are going to sit down at the table and eat all you want and say, "In Jesus' name, I command the calories to leave." That is *Foolishness*, and it is not going to work. You cannot keep eating and not get fat. You will get fatter and fatter if you keep on eating fattening foods. You are going to have to discipline yourself and bring your body under. Think about what you are doing to your body. That body does not belong to you. It is God's house. That body is the real temple of God. Not the brick and mortar that we call "the church." You need to be careful what you do to your body.

10

Believing God Not To Have Babies

Here is another area where a lot of young Christians make a mistake. They think that they are going to have sexual intercourse, and not have any babies. That is *Foolishness*. Galatians 6:7 says, "Be not deceived; God is not mocked: for whatsoever a man soweth, that shall he also reap." That means if you do the thing that produces babies, unless you do something to interrupt it, you are going to have babies. I have known of some who have prayed that they would not have any babies. They didn't take any precautionary measures and they had babies, and wondered why. They have said, "The Lord gave me this baby!"

The Lord didn't give you that baby. You got that baby yourself. You do the thing that produces babies, and you are going to have babies. Have you ever seen a farmer go out and plant corn and reap a whole field of watermelons? No! You are going to reap what you sow! If you sow babies, you are going to have a baby harvest. That's right. You can pray all you want, and say, "I'm going to pray in Jesus' name!" That's not *Faith*, that's *Foolishness*.

Now there are ways to do it that would be consistent with the Word of God. There are also some ways that I don't particularly believe are consistent with God's Word, but you are going to have to use some discretion. If you think that you are going to do your thing and just pray it away, that won't work. There are many I know of, who have babies right now because of that kind of foolish thinking. "I ain't gonna use nothing! I ain't gonna use precautions. I'm just gonna believe God!"

Yeah! You'd better start believing God for the milk to feed those babies you are going to have. That is not going to work. You reap what you sow. When sperm and eggs get together, you are going to have another you. Male or female — you are going to have another you! That's right!

Some young men and women who are just recently married and coming into contact with the faith message, think that you are going to believe God and not have babies.

HEY!!!! HEY!!!! HEY!!!! You had better do something, or you are going to have babies. That is *Foolishness*, that's not *Faith*. You keep sowing and you are going to reap. It's not *Faith* to go ahead and do what you want to do and pray, "She won't get pregnant!" It is like planting corn and saying, "Praise the Lord! Mark 11:24 says, 'What things soever ye desire . . . .' I desire watermelons. I believe this is going to be watermelons." No, it's not! You are going to reap what you sow. You sow corn, you are going to get corn. You want watermelons, you are going to have to plant watermelons. That's the way it works.

WHAT DO I DO?

There are many things going around in our society today, that a person could justifiably say, "What do I do?"

There are various methods to use to keep from having babies. I will not argue about this, but personally, I believe that it takes a sperm and an egg, and fertilization of that egg for conception to take place and a human life to come forth. Before that sperm and egg ever come together, there is no life as such. Because if there were, they would not have to come together, to produce a man. So, apparently, there is no life (man) until the sperm and the egg come together. When they get together, conception takes place. Then you have human life on your hands. Yes, that is a life. A fetus, if you would, and if you interfere with that life at that point, you can believe what you want, but in my humble opinion, you have committed murder.

The fetus is not fully developed, no question about that, but now life is there, and to interrupt that life now, is to kill.

There are many things you can use. You can use the rhythm method. You can use certain kinds of birth control pills. You can use the diaphram. There are various methods that are available to keep that sperm and that egg from coming together, but all of this should be done in the context of marriage. I cannot tell you what to do, but I think that we do need to think about this.

Remember: I am not God, and the best I can do is to share with you what I have seen in the Word of God. But you will have to be convinced in your own mind and in your heart about it. Don't do it because I said do it. Don't refrain from doing it just because I said it. Be convinced in your own heart, because you are the person who will have to answer to God for it. The Bible tells us in 1 Corinthians, that our bodies are the temples of the Holy Spirit, and that we are not our own. That means that I — the real me, the man on the inside is the custodian of this physical body that has been redeemed by the blood of Christ, and that I now belong to Jesus. If my body is a temple, then anything that I deliberately do to this body to hurt it, or to harm it, or to impair its operation in any way, form, or fashion, is tampering with something that does not belong to me. For instance, if I were to have an operation in some way to keep from having a baby, then I am doing something to God's property. I am taking God's property and I am interfering with its ability to function or operate in the way that it ought to operate. You know, you can get your tubes tied. You can get a vasectomy. There are several things that you can do. You could also use birth control pills of various kinds. I'm not going to tell you what to do: I cannot tell you that. But there are ways to control the situation without doing any harm to your physical body. You are going to have to make up your mind what you should do, but I think that you need to be very careful. I think that you should examine the situation and be convinced in your own mind, even about using the pill. Many people use the pill because it is easy.

I have heard some people say, "Well, I can't use this method, and I don't want to use that method. I want to take the pill, because it is easier. After all, we might decide to do our thing, and if we use these other things, we have to take time to get ourselves prepared."

What an excuse. You shouldn't be that greedy and lustful anyhow. You ought to have a little more control. You can take a few minutes. My gracious, if you are in that *bad-a-shape* that you can't even take a few minutes to get yourself prepared, you do have a problem. You mean that you can't wait another three minutes?

When you deal with some of those pills, they are making your body act abnormally. They create a false pregnancy. They make the body think that it is pregnant. They are lying to your body, by making it think that it is pregnant, so you don't conceive.

I don't believe that your body is meant to stay in that state. I am persuaded, you watch it, you mark it down that Brother Price said it: "One of these days, and it won't be long, they are going to come out with one of those 'after the fact reports,' saying, 'After 15 years, we have discovered that there are some dangerous side effects from a constant use of this or that type of pill.' " And it is going to be too late for you that have been using them for those 15 years. Anything that is so potent that it can make your body operate like it does not normally operate, and keep it in that condition for protracted periods of time has to be doing something chemically to your body. And I don't think that they really know all of the side effects. They have proven that to me over and over again, by continuing to come out with new reports on things that they thought were right. Then they used it because it was so very convenient. Let's face it: it is convenient to just drop a pill in your mouth.

I AM NOT SAYING for you to *use* pills, or for you to *not use* the pills. I am just making some observations, and as a person of Faith, and a person who operates in the Word of God, I am challenging you to seek God's guidance to find out what would be best for you to do.

YOUR BODY IS THE TEMPLE OF GOD

Keep this in mind: your body is the temple of God. And that body does not belong to you. There are ways, and you need to find the way that is going to work for you, and yet — is going to be consistent with the Word of God, in that it does not do any physical damage to your body.

Somebody says, "I don't agree with you!"

That's fine with me. I told you that in the first place. I AM NOT TELLING YOU WHAT TO DO, OR WHAT NOT TO DO! But I will tell you one thing: If you think that you can do the thing that produces babies, and pray and believe that you are not going to get pregnant, that is not *Faith*: that is *Foolishness*; you are going to get pregnant.

I gave you the illustration of the farmer planting corn and thinking and believing to get wheat. That won't work. You plant corn, you reap corn: everything produces after its kind.

The Bible says in Galatians 6:7; "Be not deceived; God is not mocked: for whatsoever a man soweth, that shall he also reap." If you sow sperm, you are going to reap babies. You need to think about these things because this is where you live. Some people have the idea that the Bible is for church, and when you leave the building, you leave the Bible there, and go on and do it your way. That is the reason that so many people are *messed up:* doing it their way. Do it God's way and you will come out on top. So use some wisdom and keep these things in mind and I believe you will be able to live a happy, victorious and productive life. Don't get in bondage, the whole idea is to set you free. All I am saying is to think about what you are doing to your body, because this body does not belong to you. It is God's house. This body is the real temple of God: not the brick and mortar that we call the church. We need to be careful about what we do with and to this body.

If you have sexual intercourse, and you are not doing anything to prevent babies, you are going to have babies, unless there is something wrong with you: unless you are sterile, or something like that. But all things being equal, you will have babies.

11

Claiming A Particular Husband, Or wife

Mark 11:24 says, "Therefore I say unto you. What thing soever ye desire, when ye pray, believe that ye receive them, and ye shall have them."

Some will read the above Scripture and say, "That's it! Brother Price! The Bible says, 'What things soever I desire . . . .' and I desire that this man be my husband." Or "I desire that woman to be my wife." That is not what that Scripture verse is saying at all. Nowhere in the Bible does God ever give you authority over somebody else's will. You may want her, but she may not want you.

There was a situation in Chrenshaw Christian Center, that I know of very well. A woman walked up to a man and said, "I claim you as my husband. You are going to be my husband, and there ain't nothing you can do about it." That is not *Faith:* that's *Presumption.* Most women want a husband and most men want a wife, and that is scriptural, and right. But you cannot claim a particular person per se. The other person's will is involved. That is *Foolishness,* and *Presumption:* it will not work.

When Jesus said, "What things soever ye deisre . . . ." that never includes, nor does it refer to something that will override somebody else's will. He or she may not want you. They may not even want to be married, and God is not going to force that person's will just because you desire that. That's not *Faith:* it's *Foolishness* to try that. Besides that, you may get something that you do not want.

THERE IS A RIGHT WAY TO CLAIM
A HUSBAND, OR WIFE

If I could ask some of the readers of this book: "You remember when you thought that you could not live without him, or her, and now you wish that you had never seen the one to whom you are married?"

You would answer that you wish you had never seen that rascal! That is right. You would say, "No, if I had to do it again, I wouldn't even attempt to look, because looks are deceiving."

All you see is the outward exterior anyway. God knows what is in their hearts, and He knows what is inside of you.

If you are going to claim a husband or wife, I would advise you to do this: Say, "Lord, I want a wife (husband) that will fulfill all my spiritual and physical needs. I believe that I receive according to Mark 11:24." Then I would begin to thank God for it and trust God to bring that person into my life. And I would know it when she (he) came.

In the natural, all you can do is look on the outside anyway. And you know that everything that glitters is not gold. I have seen very beautiful women, in terms of physical beauty, just nice to look at, but something else to live with. Oooooh! Awful! Horrible, terrible wives. They couldn't cook; couldn't do anything. And I have seen some who didn't look so beautiful outwardly, but they just made fabulous wives. Beauty is just skin deep anyway. The real beauty is the beauty that comes from within and shines through to the outside.

Now, I am not saying that you shouldn't have a pretty wife, or a handsome husband: you can have that too. But let God bring that person into your life. He knows what will fit you better. If you just go around basing everything on what you see; saying, "I claim him. I claim her:" that is *Foolishness*, because someone else's will is involved.

When Jesus says, "Therefore I say unto you; What things soever ye desire . . . ." You can desire a husband, or a wife, but you cannot desire that man particularly, or that woman, because He does not give you authority over somebody else's will. That is *Foolishness* and *Presumption*. It just won't work. If you want a husband, or if you want a wife, and you want to use your faith to believe for it you can use Mark 11:24, but not to override another person's will.

Don't say, "I claim Mary Jane as my wife." Mary Jane may not want you as her husband.

You believe for the husband or the wife; put your order in, then leave it to God to bring that person across your path. Then you will get the right one. You won't have to play *Russian Roulette* like some folks I know. That is not Faith when you say, "You are going to be my wife. I claim you in the name of Jesus. And there is nothing that you can do about it!" That is *Foolishness;* that is *Presumption*, that is not *Faith*.

MORE WOMEN DO THIS THAN MEN

As a pastor, I have found that women seem to be the ones to do this more than men. I get more feedback from women making that kind of statement. Ladies, that is not *Faith*, and it won't work. You will come up with the short end of the stick. You had better put your order in, and just claim your husband in the name of Jesus. And then believe God that you receive him, and stop looking. Stop hunting around. Just go ahead and seek first the kingdom of God. And the Lord will bring the right person across your path. Always remember this: you may not be ready for that man of your dreams. There may be a little fixing up that has to go on inside of you so that you will be ready for him.

THEN WITH THE MEN!

It seems like the men always want to marry the virgins. When it comes to getting married, they want the untouched, unspotted, virgin.

Have you ever stopped to think that maybe she wants a virgin too? Doesn't she deserve a virgin too? What makes you think that she wants a used model? She wants a brand new showroom-fresh-model, just like you do. It isn't fair for you to expect that on her end, and you are not giving it yourself. AMEN!

Mark 11:24 is saying, "Sure, you can have the things that you desire, but never at the expense of somebody else's will." God is not going to let you exercise authority over anybody else's will. So when it comes to this business of claiming husbands and wives, you should not claim some specific individual. You should claim that husband or wife: put your order in, and believe God that you have received it. Don't say, "I want this one, that one, or the other," because that may not be the best one for you, and besides that, he or she may not want you. And if that person doesn't want you, God is not going to change his, or her will, just to accommodate you. That is a misuse of Scripture, and it is getting over into the realm of *Presumption*. That is not *Faith*, and it will not work. God is not going to honor that; so you had better change your praying if that is what you are doing.

Stop saying, "I have my eye on him." Or "I have my eye on her." If that is what you are doing, you had better get your eye off them and on the Word of God. Seek ye first the kingdom of God . . . ., and use your faith properly, because that is not *Faith*, that is *Presumption*, and it will not work.

I HAVE CLAIMED A HUSBAND (WIFE) BUT I HAVE NOT RECEIVED

There is another aspect to this business of husband and wife claiming, that I need to address myself to. Some have been claiming husbands and wives for a long time, and they haven't received yet. They are wondering what is wrong. I think that the Bible gives us a little clarification here, and we need to examine this, because it is very important to us.

In James 4:1-3, we read; "From whence come wars and fightings among you? come they not hence, even of your lusts that war in your members? Ye lust, and have not: ye kill, and desire to have, and cannot obtain: ye fight and war, yet ye have not, because ye ask not. Ye ask, and receive not, because ye ask amiss, that ye may consume it upon your lusts." There is such a thing as asking for something and having the wrong motive. You can be doing the right thing, but have the wrong motive. To claim a husband or a wife for the wrong motive is really not right. He said, "You ask and receive not because you ask amiss." In other words, your motive is not right. "You ask amiss that you may consume it upon your lust."

Now, when I say that you can put your order in for a husband or wife, what you really ought to do is to claim a husband, or wife, and then leave it up to God. You have claimed the husband. You have claimed the wife: now leave it up to God to bring that person into your life. Some have gone off the deep end, and they are claiming; "I want her to be 39-24-38," or whatever, and they are really not operating in *Faith*. They are operating out of *lust.* What does the size of a woman's breasts have to do with the happiness of marriage? We have got lust on our minds. What difference does it make if she is 39 inches or 37? Is two inches going to make you happy? Is that what makes a good marriage? Some have said, "He has to have 25 inch thighs, and 15 inch calves."

The size of the organs, whatever organs we are talking about, does not determine the happiness of marriage. And when you are really that concerned about whether it is 30 or 39 inches, you are not operating out of a desire, just to have a wife, you are operating out of a desire to have some kind of physical play toy. Your marriage is already doomed to destruction, because your motive is not right in the first place. She has to be a certain color, and have a certain kind of hair, and be a certain height. Hair has nothing to do with you being happy. I know some people who have the prettiest hair that you would ever want to see: the most beautiful people, yet they have the worst marriage in the world. I also know some folks, on the other hand who are bald-headed and have the most beautiful marriage going. They don't have any hair! Don't you think that God knows that you don't want some ugly worn out something, be it male or female. Don't you think that God has enough sense to know that? You trusted Him with your salvation. You trusted Him to write your name down in the Lamb's Book of Life, why can't you trust Him for a husband, or wife?

Why does she have to be 38 or whatever?

"If it ain't that, I don't want it." You can see right there you are in lust. You don't desire a husband, or wife: you are looking for some kind of flesh toy to play with.

Friend, what you look like outwardly, whether your hair is long, short, nappy, kinky, straight, blond, black, brunette, or you have no hair at all: whether you are tall, or short: whether you are 22 or 39 inches in the chest, none of that automatically is going to make a happy marriage. If you don't get beyond that, you are doomed already, even before you start, because marriage is based on more than sex.

In our society, we blow sex so much out of proportion that we think that it is the great determining factor. She thinks she is going to be happy because he has a certain size thigh, or a certain size this or that. How do you know that that is going to make you happy? Besides, what guarantee do you have that after you marry him, that he is going to stay the same size anyhow? I know a person in the church that I pastor, that I went to high school with. A beautiful young lady, physically: short, slim, and trim. The person is still a very beautiful person to me, but she has — over the years, because of many different circumstances permitted herself to get five sizes bigger than she was then. And now, she doesn't look as good in her clothes.

Just because he is that size now, does not mean that he is going to stay that way. And just because she is that size now, doesn't mean that she is going to stay that way. So what are you going to do after she has your third kid? Before she had all those babies she may have been standing out there nice and firm at 38 inches. But after those babies, she may not have that nice shape.

It's true. You know. This is where we live. If somebody had talked to you about this before you married, you might not be in the problems that you are now in. This is life; we need to face the facts and the realities of life. Marriage should not be based on physical dimensions. Your happiness is not guaranteed because of physical dimensions: that is *Foolishness:* that is not trusting God.

LEARN TO TRUST YOUR HEAVENLY FATHER

You are going to have to learn to trust your heavenly Father, and get your mind off of physical dimensions, and looks, and start seeking the kingdom of God first. Put your order in, but not that silly stuff: talking about, "He has to have an ear lobe so much higher than his cheekbones, and his hair has to be this, and he has to have a mustache; he has to be so much across the shoulders etc., etc., etc.!" Get off that! Say, "Father God, I want a husband, and You know that I want one who looks nice. You know I don't want to marry King Kong, and I don't want Godzilla either. But I am going to trust you Lord. And I claim a husband (wife) in the name of Jesus, and I believe that I receive according to Mark 11:24." Then leave it up to God to bring the man or woman into your life, because, remember: you are the result of a certain set of circumstances. You have your own peculiar psychological make up: you are the product of a particular environment, and history, and tradition, and of family relationships. Many times, you think that you want this, but would you fit with him or her? Doesn't he or she have something to say about it?

Maybe you are a size 24, looking like a "who'd—a—thought—it," and you put in an order for a "tall, dark, and handsome." What makes you think he wants you?

You don't even think about that. "I want. I want!" What about you? Maybe you are not fixed up for that kind of man. Maybe that is why your prayers have not been answered. You want "tall, dark, and handsome," but you are "short, fat, and ugly." I'm not calling names. I am simply trying to get you to see the truth. We need to be careful about this. What makes you think that he or she wants you, anyhow?

That may be why you are having such a hard time getting a husband, or wife. You may be asking foolishly. Just put your order in and claim a husband, or wife. That way, you won't have to look for one any more. Claim it in the name of Jesus and believe that you have received. Leave it up to your heavenly Father.

I MADE UP MY MIND, BUT GOD KNEW THE KIND OF GIRL I NEEDED

I did that! I had my mind (This was before I even knew about faith, or claiming anything, even before I was a Christian.) all made up as to the kind of girl I was going to marry, if — in fact, I ever got married. In reality, marriage was the furthest thing from my mind, but I did have some remote thoughts about it. There was no point in getting married when I could play. That was my attitude. That was the way I felt, and man, I was playing! I was having a good time. I had no immediate plans to marry. No! I was foot-loose and fancy-free! And when I did start thinking seriously about getting married, I had it all in my mind the kind of girl I was going to marry, and just what she was going to look like. She had to be a certain color, she had to have a certain texture of hair. I had made up my mind. I did not know that God would have anything to do with it, but that is what I had in my mind. I thought that that was going to make me happy.

My wife had prayed, after a fashion, and the Lord worked the thing out as far as the physical things were concerned, even though they didn't work out exactly as I had envisioned them. But I wouldn't trade the woman the Lord gave me for a million dollars. I thought she had to be a certain complexion, she had to be a certain color, and that would insure happiness. I still got the best and I tell her that. I wouldn't trade my family for a million dollars. My wife is not the color I thought I wanted in a wife, but let me tell you, I have a happy, happy marriage. And I wouldn't trade that woman for anything! I am not kidding! Good looking! And she can cook! She can put the pots on — yes! I am trying to show you that the complexion of one's skin doesn't make a happy marriage. That is *Foolishness*, not *Faith*.

Let me say this, because I run into this situation quite often. There are some black women, and this goes for men also, that think that the only man that can make them happy is a white man. That is *Foolishness!*

You won't have a happy marriage just because his skin is white, and you don't have to have a bad marriage because his skin is black. The color of your skin does not have a thing in the world to do with you having a happy marriage. I have seen some miserable folks that were white: I have seen some miserable folks that were black: I have seen some miserable folks that were oriental: and I have seen some miserable folks that were Spanish. I have seen some miserable people period! The color of your skin does not guarantee you happiness. I want you to understand that.

It is better for you if you want the man (woman) that God knows is best for you. I am not saying that I believe that God has a great big chart up in heaven with all the males listed, and all the females listed, and God already — before we ever came into being had matched them up as to which ones were going to be with whom. I don't believe that, but I do believe that God knows the best person for you. That is what I am saying. I believe that God knows best, the person with the kind of qualities that will match yours so that you will flow together and not be butting heads. I don't believe that God has a man and a woman picked out for everybody, without you having anything to do with it. But I do believe that God knows what is best for you. He knows what will work best with you. If you will just claim the husband (wife), and leave the statistics to God. That will release your faith, and open the door for God to bring the person into your life. And when He brings that person into your life, that person is going to fit you like a tailor-made suit.

It is *Foolishness* to say, "Child, I am going to have him. And he is going to be white. He is going to have freckles." Or "He is going to have short hair." Or "long hair. He is going to be this size, that size, or the other." That is *Foolishness*. And it could be that you want to consume it on your lust, as we read in James. That may be why you have not received. It is not *Faith*, just because you go out and claim somebody. You should let God bring the person to you.

ADAM DID'T COMPLAIN ABOUT THE WIFE THAT GOD GAVE HIM

We read in Genesis 2:21-25, "And the Lord God caused a deep sleep to fall upon Adam, and he slept; and he took one of his ribs, and closed up the flesh instead thereof; And the rib, which the Lord God had taken from man, made he a woman, and brought her unto the man. And Adam said, This is now bone of my bones, and flesh of my flesh: she shall be called Woman, because she was taken out of Man. Therefore, shall a man leave his father and his mother, and shall cleave unto his wife: and they shall be one flesh. And they were both naked, the man and his wife, and were not ashamed."

Now, the point that I want to bring out is this: you noticed that Adam did not complain about what God had made him. We have no indications at all that Adam was unhappy or dissatisfied with what God had created for him. All I am saying is that if Adam could have that much confidence in God, you can have that much confidence in God, and believe that He is going to bring the kind of person into your life, male or female, that is going to be best suited for you, and who you will be best suited for. And therefore, will produce for you a most happy marriage, and a most beautiful blessed relationship.

So I don't believe necessarily that it is *Faith* when you go out and just claim a person. "I claim him. He has to be this size . . . ." That is *Foolishness*. When I say, put in a claim, I mean, tell God what you want. If you want a husband, tell Him you want a husband, but I really believe that you ought to back off of the statistics because you think that is what is going to make you happy, but you have no guarantee that once you marry, you won't have a problem on your hands. A lot of times the things you think will make you happy, don't really make you happy at all.

You can trust your Father God. After all, He saved you: He filled you with the Holy Ghost: He has your name written down in the Lamb's Book of Life: He is blessing you as you are operating in His Word, and I think it would be best just to claim the husband, or wife in the name of Jesus, and leave the rest to God. He knows you don't want to marry King King or Godzilla, and I think there are plenty of people to go around for everybody. Some people don't want to marry. But if you do desire to marry, I think that if you are going to use your faith in the area of claiming a husband or wife, then you should just claim the husband or the wife and leave the statistics up to God. Trust Him. If you are going to trust Him with your eternal salvation, you ought to be able to trust Him for a husband or wife. You should just believe that you have received, and stop looking or shopping around. Because if you believe that you have received, you don't need to shop. There is no point in looking now, because God will bring the person to you, and you will know it when this happens.

When you start acting on or claiming a certain person, you are getting into *Foolishness* and *Presumption*, and you are getting ready to get your head cut off, because you are going to get something that you don't want.

Many times, I have sat across the desk and heard the words, "I wish I had never seen that woman! She is driving me crazy." But he thought that he couldn't live without her, the same as she thought that she couldn't live without him. And now he has found out that he can't live with her.

The point is this. Seek first the kingdom of God, and put your claim in for a husband or wife. Believe that you have received according to Mark 11:24, and leave the size, color, dimensions, and statistics to your heavenly Father.

12

Finances In The Home Situation

What about writing checks when you have no money in the bank to cover them, and believing that God will supernaturally put the money there? Is that *Faith*, *Foolishness*, or *Presumption?*

I know a man who is a minister of the Gospel, and he is out in the teaching ministry. He teaches around the country, just as I do, and he is a very prominent man in the ministry of the Word today. I heard a video tape of his some years ago, and he was saying that when he first got hold of the faith message, he had acted very foolishly concerning finances. He had a lot of bills and he was going to use his faith and claim that he could write checks and send them in, and believe that God was going to supernaturally put the money in the bank to cover the checks. Well, you know what happened. Every one of them bounced! That is not *Faith*.

If someone writes you a check and doesn't have any money to cover it, that is dishonest. You could not do that as an exercise of your faith and expect God to honor it. Do you know why? Because it is dishonest, unless you post date a check and tell the person that you give the check to that it will not be good until this date. If you write a check and give it to someone before you have the money in the bank to cover it, you are absolutely being dishonest because when you give a person a check, you are saying that there is money in the bank to cover it. Isn't that what a check is for? It takes the place of money. So if you write a check and hand it to a person, that person assumes, unless you tell him otherwise, that there is money in the bank to cover that check.

That is not *Faith*. That is *Presumption* and *Foolishness*. That will not work, and you will get into serious trouble. You are going to ruin you own good credit, and your own good name, and you will bring dishonor to the kingdom of God, if you do this. That is not *Faith*. You shouldn't write any checks until you have the money in the bank to cover them.

This business about writing a check and getting to the bank before the check clears to put the money in, is being dishonest. When you write that check and hand it to a person, you are saying to that person, "I have money in the bank to cover this check." And if you don't have money in the bank to cover it, I don't care what you plan to have in the bank (What happens if they have a fire in the company where you work and the thing burns down?), if you don't get that money in there, you will be messed up. And you lied to the man, because the money was not in the bank. If you don't have any money in the bank, you don't have any business writing a check. Somebody gave me a check one day. We were in Santa Paula, California, and this man said, "I want to buy a couple of your books, but I don't have any money in the bank: I am going to post date this check. Don't put it in the bank until then."

Fine, wonderful. I could receive that. I could agree with that. But if I had put it in the bank before he deposited some money in the bank, it would have bounced. There would not have been any money in there to cover the amount of the check.

If you think that you are using *Faith* and you just go out and write a bunch of checks, and send them in, and there is no money in the bank to cover them, that is not

Faith: that's *Foolishness.* God is not going to supernaturally drop some money in the bank. The only way that money is going to get into the bank is when you make a deposit, or somebody else makes a deposit to your account. Is that *Faith, Foolishness,* Or *Presumption?* You tell me!

Is it *Faith,* the fact that I am going to believe God to pay all my bills off, and I go out and write all of those checks before I put the money in the bank? That is not *Faith:* that is *Foolishness.*

A WAY TO USE YOUR FAITH

I do know of a situation where a man used his faith this way. He sat down and wrote out all of the checks to cover his bills, and claimed the money to cover them. He wrote his checks out, but did not date them, nor send them out, until the money came in to cover each check. When the money came in, he put the dates on the checks and sent them out. That is all right. You can do that. But when you write a check to someone and you hand it to them, you are saying that the money is in the bank to cover that check. And if it isn't in the bank, that is not *Faith:* that is *Foolishness* and *Presumption,* and it is a downright lie. You need to get it together and all things being equal, you should know how much money you have in your checking account.

Now, I realize a human error can happen occasionally, but you have to admit that banks really don't make that many mistakes on your personal checking account. I have been doing business with the same bank for many years, and I do not remember them having ever made a mistake on my checking account. Week after week after week, you go to the bank, and it is very seldom that they ever make a mistake with your account. You multiply that by thousands of other accounts, and I think that is a pretty good record.

If they should make a mistake, you will have to admit that it is not that often. Usually, when that check comes back marked #6 — *Insufficient funds,*" it is because there were insufficient funds.

Don't think it's *Faith* just because you write a check and you are going to believe God to put the money in the bank supernaturally. That is ridiculous. That is not going to work. That is not *Faith:* that is *Presumption,* and *Foolishness.*

HOUSEHOLD MONEY AND TITHE PAYING

Another aspect that we need to consider is whether or not wives or husbands should take household money and pay tithes when the husband or wife objects to it. I have heard people say, "Well, this is *my money,* and this is *her money.*" There is no such thing as *my money,* or *her money:* it is our money. If you are married, and you are husband and wife, and you are talking about "my money," it should be "our money."

"Yes, but I'm the one who is working."

Come on. The Bible says that you are "one." When a man and woman leave their father and mother and the two join themselves together, they are *one* in the sight of God, and if only one of them is working, every nickel, quarter, or dime that that working person brings home is for both. That money is as much hers as it is his, and it is as much his as it is hers. Talking about your money as your money! The only money that is your money is the money that the two of you agree to take out of the pay check each week to be your spending money. That is *your money* and *her money.* But when the check comes in, that money belongs to the household, and you are getting a rotten deal if that man isn't bringing that money home, Sister. You are getting a rotten deal. Unfortunately, I find that to be true too often. Men do their wives that way, and that is really dirty or rotten to treat your wife like that. Some women don't even know where their husbands work! And they don't even know how much money the rascal makes. They never even see one of the pay checks. Boy, that really gives her a "great sense of security." That really gives her a "feeling of belonging." That is a *bum deal,* if you ask me. That's what it is!

You may be a Christian woman and you say, "I am going to act in faith. I want to tithe."

Don't take the grocery money and tithe out of it. If he is a non-believer, that is one of the best ways to keep him from becoming a believer. Fooling with his money, Honey. That is not the way to do it. Don't you think that God knows that he is a non-believer? Don't you think that God knows that he is against tithing? You don't prove anything by taking the grocery money and tithing, or giving it in offerings instead of using the money for what the man gave it to you for. That is not *Faith;* that is *Foolishness* and *Presumption.*

"But the Bible says I ought to tithe." That is if you are working or have some money of your own. But the grocery money is not your income. That money is to be used for running the household, and you will make that non-believing husband *madder than a hornet* quicker than anything by taking the money out and spending it on something else.

My wife and I were in another city, and this little girl wanted to talk to my wife after the service was over. She was in tears, and having a fit. My wife couldn't talk to her until she wrote out a check and gave it to her. Poor silly child. She thought that she was exercising her faith by taking the grocery money and putting it in church. That is not *Faith*. Now, if he gives you a weekly allowance and you want to tithe out of that, that is perfectly proper. But you should not take household money: money to be used to pay the rent, the bills, and to buy the groceries, whatever it is, and take that and put it in the church. God does not expect you to do that. And if you do so, that is not going to make your marriage situation a happy one. It is not going to cause that man to come to Christ. That is not *Faith* when you say, "My husband does not believe in tithing, but I am going to use the grocery money and tithe anyhow! I want to tithe." Don't you think that God knows that. He will give you credit for it, even though you do not tithe. Do not take the household money and give it anyway, when you know that you husband doesn't like it. He is already talking about the preacher for getting all the money, and he is already mad about that. That is not the right thing to do. God doesn't expect you to do that. If you have a non-believing husband, you will never win him by taking that man's money and putting it into the church. Satan is going to use that to make him that much angrier against the church. Use some wisdom. That is not *Faith*. God knows your circumstances. He knows you cannot tithe, and He does not expect you to do so. You are not working in that sense: you are a housewife. You do what you are supposed to do at home. Live the Christian life before your husband. That will do more to win him than anything else. If he gives you some extra money, or something like that, you can go ahead and give it to the Lord.

God does not expect you to tithe if your husband is not in agreement with it. In fact, if two people who are Christians do not agree to tithe, you shouldn't do it: not against the other's will. You should come to some kind of compromise on what you do together and then what belongs to you, that part that is yours, you can do with it what you want to do. It is not *Faith*, just to go on and give that money in spite of your spouse's feelings on the subject. You will get yourself into a lot of trouble. You will mess up your home situation and that is not using wisdom: that is not *Faith:* that is *Foolishness*.

13

Faith Vs. Fear

As we come to the final chapter of this book, I believe that we have thoroughly covered many aspects that Christians face in their daily lives. Is it *Faith, Foolishness, Or Presumption?* I believe that we have adequately shown that when the Scripture says, "Owe no man anything except to love him . . ." (See Romans 13:8) it does not necessarily mean that you cannot buy anything on time and make monthly payments. You don't look to that as a way of getting things for the rest of your life, but you use it as a stepping stone. The faith life is a progressive development. Nobody is born a full grown physical adult, and neither is a new born again Christian fully developed in his faith walk. Spiritual babies have to grow up.

We have also talked about whether or not it is *Faith, Foolishness, Or Presumption* to not have insurance. And you have to remember that you live in an imperfect world. Insurance is a means of preventing the enemy from wiping you out financially. Just as health insurance won't prevent you from getting sick or dying, neither does automobile insurance prevent you from having wrecks. Every one is at different levels of faith. And everybody has to choose for himself or herself. All insurance does is help you keep from giving place to the devil. We have talked about many things: about husbands and wives' relationships. Even whether to claim or not to claim a husband or wife. A lot of this goes on under the guise of *Faith*, when in fact, it is really *Foolishness,* and in some instances, *Presumption.* We have talked about eating and casting out the calories, and that is *Foolishness,* because you cannot keep eating and not get fat. You will get fatter and fatter and fatter if you keep on eating fattening foods. You are going to have to discipline yourself and bring your body under.

There is one aspect that we have not talked about. And that is the subject of *fear*. *Fear* is one of the greatest things that hinders many Christian's faith. *Fear* of the dog: *fear* of the dark: *fear* of the cat: *fear* of this and that. *Fear* keeps people in bondage. 2 Timothy 1:7 says, "For God hath not given us the spirit of fear; but of power, and of love, and of a sound mind." Now that is the Word of God. You do not have the *spirit of fear*. You can permit or allow the *spirit of fear* to dominate you if you want to. But fear has no legal right to make you afraid. You can be afraid if you choose to be afraid, but you do not have to be afraid.

When *fear* rears its ugly head, you have the right and authority in the name of Jesus to point the finger of God at *fear* and say, "In the name of Jesus, I refuse to be afraid!" And until you start doing that, *fear* is going to dominate you. Because satan knows he has you running, and he will keep on harassing you in that area.

The Bible says that we have not been given the spirit of fear, so we don't have to be afraid.

YOU HAVE TO DEAL WITH THAT FEAR

For instance, if a wife has a husband who works at night and she is afraid of the dark, she does not want to stay at home by herself. So she prays and believes that her husband will get a daytime job. That won't work because you see, you are not dealing with the *fear*. You are trying to change the circumstances, so that he works in the daytime when you are not afraid, instead of at night. You need to stop and realize that you have not dealt with the *fear*. You still have the same *fear*, and that *fear* is still dominating you.

Any time you pray in contradiction to the Word of God, it will not work. That is not *Faith*. That is *Foolishness*. Yea, even *Presumption*.

You can learn to overcome fear. You can use the Word of God to overcome it. It is not Faith to pray that they put your husband on a daytime job so that he won't have to be away at night. If this were true, in our relationship, I would not even go anywhere in the ministry.

MY WIFE HAD A FEAR OF THE DARK

I did not even know it; she kept it to herself, but my wife had a fear of the dark. She was afraid to get out of the bed and go to the toilet in the middle of the night. That is how fearful she was. She would never sleep, any time when I was away from home. If I didn't get home until 2:00 a.m., she would not go to sleep until then. And if I did not come home that night, if I was out of town preaching, although she did not tell me, she would stay awake the whole night: never closing her eyes. *Fear had her.* She would hear sounds or noises, and she would think that somebody was going to break into the house on her.

Fear is dominating. Well, she did not pray that God would stop sending me away to preach. She did not pray that God would stop causing invitations to come to me that would keep me out somewhere ministering the Word of God.

She found out that the Bible is true. She found out that *she had not been given the spirit of fear, but of power, and of love, and of a sound mind.* She found out that Jesus Himself said, In Luke 10:19; "Behold, I give unto you power to tread on serpents and scorpions, and over all the power of the enemy: and nothing shall by any means hurt you." She found out that the Word of God said that *whatever we bind on earth, is bound in heaven, and whatever we loose on earth is loosed in heaven.* She found out in the name of Jesus, you can cast these spirits out. And she began to use her faith. She began to take authority over *fear*. She began to say, "I will not be afraid. I will not stay awake all night. I will not be afraid; nobody can break in on me because the angels of the Lord are encamped around and about me. Greater is He that is in me, than he that is in the world, and I don't have to be afraid." She took authority over that thing. She did not pray that God would stop sending me out at night to preach the Word of God: that is *Presumption* and *Foolishness.* That is not *Faith.*

If you have that kind of *fear*, you can overcome it. But you are going to have to learn how to stand against it with the Word of God. She overcame that *fear*. She is afraid of nothing now. She gets in that bed, and in fact, if I don't get to her quickly, she will be asleep. She took the Word of God and overcame the *fear*.

It is *Foolishness* to pray, "Lord, put him on a day time job." You have not dealt with the *fear*. If you say, "Lord, send me by bus instead of by airplane. I'm scared to fly." You are still letting *fear* dominate you. That is not *Faith*, that is *Foolishness*, and *Presumption*. Learn to take the Word of God and learn to rise above these situations. *We have not been given the spirit of fear, but of love, and of power, and of a sound mind.* You don't have to be afraid of anything: not a dog, a frog, a toad, an ant, a person, a demon, satan, or anybody else. You do not have to be afraid. There is no *fear* for the man who knows how to walk in line with God's Word.

FAITH, FOOLISHNESS, OR PRESUMPTION?
YOU BE THE JUDGE!